The Roles of the Woman

Marshall Osborne, Jr.

authorHOUSE®

AuthorHouse™
1663 Liberty Drive
Bloomington, IN 47403
www.authorhouse.com
Phone: 1 (800) 839-8640

Published by AuthorHouse 01/28/2019

ISBN: 978-1-5462-7542-8 (sc)
ISBN: 978-1-5462-7543-5 (e)

Library of Congress Control Number: 2019900285

Print information available on the last page.

All scriptures of reference are taken from King James Version, The Open Bible, Expanded Edition, Copyright 1985 by Thomas Nelson, Inc.

Contents

Acknowledgments

The author wishes to express special thanks and appreciation to his son, Garrick Maurice Osborne, for designing, and producing the cover of this book and the previous three books. You have been exceptionally talented and patience while I wrote the manuscripts for the books. And when I needed your expertise, you were right on time. I continually pray that God will forever bless you in your walk with him, with love your dad.

Introduction

Now behold the woman! In the "Roles of the Man," we read that man failed to own up to what God wanted him to be simply because of woman. Eve, who became disobedient to God's commandments, caused the fall of man. Since that time, we have seen the rise of women to the dominant role through many generations. Is this what an help meet was made for? Is today's woman doing her God-given roles? Can we imagine women being the weaker vessels looking at the plight of man? And lastly who shall answer to all this? That's why it is very important to understand "The Roles of the Woman."

> *And the Lord God said, It is not good that the man should be alone; I will make him an help meet for him.*
>
> *And the Lord God caused a deep sleep to fall upon Adam, and he slept: and he took one of his ribs, and closed up the flesh instead thereof;*
>
> *And the rib, which the Lord God had taken from man, made he a woman, and brought her unto the man.*
>
> *And Adam said, This is now bone of my bones, and flesh of my flesh: she shall be called Woman, because she was taken out of Man.* (Genesis 2:18, 21-23)

CHAPTER 1

The Woman

As we look at the creation of woman, it is uniquely clear that woman was not created like man, but from man. The man was made from the dust of the earth. The woman was made from the rib of man and because she was "bones of Adam's bones, and flesh of Adam's flesh," she also must return to the dust.

God had observed the loneliness of man and has seen fit to help man overcome this loneliness by making a help meet for him in a way that she will cause him good memories and days. Loneliness, today, should not be a part of man's life because of woman. But as we see in society today, loneliness is not only in man's life but also in the woman's life. Instead of being each other's remedy for loneliness, we have seen each entity drowned in loneliness. How? Romans (1:24-28) says:

> *"Wherefore God also gave them up to uncleanness through the lusts of their own hearts, to dishonour their own bodies between themselves: Who changed the truth of God into a lie, and worshipped and served the creature more than the Creator, who is blessed for ever. Amen. For this cause God gave them up unto vile affections: for even their women did change the natural use into that which is against nature: And likewise also the men, leaving the natural use of the woman, burned in their lust one toward another; men with men working that which is unseemly, and receiving in themselves that recompence of their error which was meet. And even as they did not like to retain God in their*

knowledge, God gave them over to a reprobate mind, to do those things which are not convenient;"

What God had tried to prevent, man and his influential adversary have seen fit to keep in place. Man by God was given lead way to go out and cleave unto him his wife. But not all men will do this. Does this pertain to woman also? God made woman to be man's remedy from being alone. Thus, we find that every woman being born is destined to marry or has a mate. She is the other half to help replenish the earth and her roles are very important to man and God.

"Therefore shall a man leave his father and his mother, and shall cleave unto his wife: and they shall be one flesh."

How far had we come and now turned back into sin? Does God know best, or does man know best? Proverbs (18:22) says,

"Whoso findeth a wife findeth a good thing, and obtaineth favour of the Lord."

As a result of seeking him a wife, a man will find a woman that will be a good thing for him. And because he did as God commanded, then he and his wife will obtain favour of God.

I can recall the first time I met my wife in a high school laboratory. She was a beautiful and quiet individual. Something inside of me came to life. I had several girlfriends at that time, but nothing ever clicked inside as it did with this young lady. I can bear witness with the scripture, *man shall cleave unto his wife.* This young lady who I had not known caught my interest and somewhat my heart. I couldn't stop looking over at her as she did her laboratory experiment. I saw my high school chemistry teacher at the front of the class. I immediately went over to greet her and to let her know my status in college. I had a break in college and was home for awhile and I wanted to visit my old high school and see my chemistry teacher who was very instrumental in my majoring in chemistry at South Carolina State College, which is now South Carolina State University. As I made my way toward her, my eyes saw the love of my life. I passed by this young lady, but I had to look her way again before reaching the teacher. Once I reached the teacher, we greeted each other and exchanged some small talk, then she asked a favor of me while I was there. And that was to oversee the class while she runs an errand. Boy! This gave me an opportunity to meet this young lady that had me transfixed. I had to get to know her or simply meet her. She seemed to be a stimulus for me, not as a sexual partner, but one that will make good memories and days together. I found the reason to meet her through her wallet being taken by another male classmate. I took the wallet from him and being curious peeked into the wallet for her name and telephone number. God must have been in the midst of it, because everything was there to see who she was and how to get in touch with her after school. I gave her back the wallet but kept her little coin pouch just to have some leverage to see her again.

Furthermore, I found the nerves to call and ask her out for an ice cream date one weekend. She agreed. I met her family and some of her relatives at that time and felt good about her, because she was a virtuous woman. I can recall a scripture in Proverbs (12:4) which says;

> *"A virtuous woman is a crown to her husband: but she that maketh ashamed is as rottenness in his bones."*

I thought I was a king and she was the queen as we drove to that ice cream parlor. It was also funny because we weren't alone in the car. Her family had insisted that if we go anywhere, we would take her nieces and nephew, the three amigos as we called them at that time. It really didn't matter to me, because I was with my companion and the wife of my youth. Malachi (2:14-15) says,

> *"Yet ye say, Wherefore? Because the Lord hath been witness between thee and the wife of thy youth, against whom thou hast dealt treacherously: yet is she thy companion, and the wife of thy covenant. And did not he make one? Yet had he the residue of the spirit. And wherefore one? That he might seek a godly seed. Therefore take heed to your spirit, and let none deal treacherously against the wife of his youth."*

In my mind I was thinking, I'll be please to have her dwell with me as husband and wife. Today, this is a reality. We have been happily married for approximately forty-seven years. We both have striven to live as Christ's Word says and have reaped the benefits with each other. God requires us to live with one another according to knowledge. I Peter (3:7) says,

> *"Likewise, ye husbands, dwell with them according to knowledge, giving honour unto the wife, as unto the weaker vessel, and as being heirs together of the grace of life; that your prayers be not hindered."*

CHAPTER 2

The Wife

God saw that it was not good that a man should be alone and set out to make him an help meet (Genesis (2:18). Thus, the woman was made and brought unto Adam for his wife. The wife for God's purpose is a married woman to a husband. We realize today that this is not the case in all marriages. Laws have been passed to supersede God's commandments to allow "woman and woman" and "man and man" to marry. This perverse generation has turned away from God's commandments and made its own laws to govern marriage. Those who believe that marriage is between a man and a woman can delight in these words of admonishment and comfort.

It is expected of a woman to rise to the role of "wife" when she leaves her mother and father and takes on a spouse. Genesis (3:16) says:

> *"Unto the woman he said, I will greatly multiply thy sorrow and thy conception; in sorrow thou shalt bring forth children; and thy desire shall be to thy husband, and he shall rule over thee."*

We can clearly see the different between God's Word and man's word. There is no way a "man and man" marriage can bring forth children. Nor can a "woman and woman" marriage bring forth children. A woman or wife can't be called a husband so that she can rule over her. Likewise, for the man or husband cannot be called a wife so that she can bring forth children. Our leaders have really damned the souls of many people with their laws on marriages and divorces.

The wife's duties toward the husband should be:

- To submit to him,
- To be in submission to him,
- To give reverence to him,
- To love him,
- To learn from him,
- To be trustworthy to him,
- To love her children,
- To be chaste, and
- To be keepers at home for him.

All of these requirements for the woman and the wife are commanded by God. From creation, God had set standards for each: roles of the man and woman. He expects each individual to obey and abide in his Word. He (God) says in Ephesians (5:22-24) for the wife:

> *"Wives, submit yourselves unto your own husbands, as unto the Lord. For the husband is the head of the wife, even as Christ is the head of the church: and he is the saviour of the body. Therefore as the church is subject unto Christ, so let the wives be to their own husbands in every thing."*

However, here we can understand that God wants the wife to be willing to obey the husband in all things. But due to our environment today whereby we have adamant women rights' and women's abuse organizations, our wives are no more submitting or in submission. Do I blame them? No. The majority of the wives being portrayed in our media are not faith abiding women. But women who profess that they are of elite status, thereby not trying to live by God's Word. "The Real Housewives of______" reality shows are prime examples of wives who are not in submission to their husbands and live not according to the Word of God.

Most reality shows are the propaganda of the adversary. He, Satan, uses these means to influence the mind of our innocent ones and get them off the Word of God so that they use their own knowledge instead of the knowledge of God. Likewise, he gives them a new norm other than that God has put forth. Have you seen how subtle they programmed homosexuality in the commercials and programs these days? It looks like every station has blended in the new norm. What is the new norm? It's okay to be gay and/or a transsexual. The saying is that God made them that way. God did not make individuals with this type of life style. Only, Satan, who has twisted the minds and hearts of individuals can say and get man to say such absurd things. God is quite displeased with this type life style and behavior. Who shall pay for this arrogance?

Similarly, I Peter (3:1-6) says:

> *"Likewise, ye wives, be in subjection to your own husbands; that, if any obey not the word, they also may without the word be won by the conservation of the wives; While they behold your chaste conversation coupled with fear. Whose adorning let it not be that outward adorning of plaiting the hair, and of wearing of gold, or of putting on of apparel; But let it be the hidden man of the heart, in that which is not corruptible, even the ornament of a meek and quiet spirit, which is in the sight of God of great price. For after this manner in the old time the holy women also, who trusted in God, adorned themselves, being in subjection unto their own husbands: Even as Sara obeyed Abraham, calling him lord: whose daughters ye are, as long as ye do well, and are not afraid with any amazement."*

It somewhat puzzles me to know if Eve had been totally submissive to Adam would this world be any different. I've come to the conclusion that it would not be much different. How did I arrive at that? Remember the people outside of the Garden of Eden were not submissive to the will of God, either. Adam and Eve had two sons in the family. When Cain left his parents and went out and married. There must have been other people on earth beside Adam and Eve. This is true if you study the book of Genesis:

> *"And Adam knew Eve his wife; and she conceived, and bare Cain, and said, I have gotten a man from the Lord. And she again bare his brother Abel. And Abel was a keeper of sheep, but Cain was a tiller of the ground. And Cain went out from the*

> *presence of the Lord, and dwelt in the land of Nod, on the east of Eden. And Cain knew his wife; and she conceived, and bare Enoch: and he builded a city, and called the name of the city, after the name of his son, Enoch."* (Genesis 4:1-2, 16-17)

Furthermore, in the fifth chapter of Genesis, you'll find the answer:

> *"This is the book of the generations of Adam. In the day that God created man, in the likeness of God made he him; Male and female created he them; and blessed them, and called their name Adam, in the day when they were created."*

This tells us that there were other people on earth beside Adam and Eve in the Garden of Eden. God had a beginning point and He began with Adam and Eve in the Garden of Eden. But outside the garden there were other Adams and Eves.

Moreover, if our wives were all of faith and striving to live faithfully as God requires, then marriage would be the holy institution He made it to be. Women today do not like to submit or give reverence to the man simply because God said so. God had made women the weaker vessels and therefore they are subject to men. Only women of God would show submissiveness, obedience, and reverence to their husbands because of the standards of God. Sarah showed reverence to her husband Abraham as stated in I Peter (3:5-6) and Ephesians (5:33):

> *"For after this manner in the old time the holy women also, who trusted in God, adorned themselves, being in subjection unto their own husbands; Even as Sara obeyed Abraham, calling him lord: whose daughters ye are, as long as ye do well, and are not afraid with any amazement."*

> *"Nevertheless let every one of you in particular so love his wife even as himself; and the wife see that she reverence her husband."*

We might have a problem with this saying due to our inability to live what God expects of us as men and women. Man doesn't know his roles and surely woman doesn't know her roles. We love some of the roles of man and woman, and the most important one is the love making role as husband and wife. No one has time to learn from one another. Yet, God wants the elderly men and women to teach the younger ones coming up so that they will know his ways and standards. Titus (2:3-5) says:

> *"The aged women likewise, that they be in behaviour as becometh holiness, not false accusers, not given to much wine, teachers of good things; That they may teach the young women to be sober, to love their husbands, to love their children. To be discreet, chaste, keepers at home, good, obedient to their own husbands, that the word of God be not blasphemed."*

Today, our young women do not want to hear what the elderly women have to say, because it sounds out of date with what the world is teaching them. They quickly will tell you that they are not ready to profess holiness and to give up their way of life for God's way. And because we do not enforce the word of God to our children, we have many rapes, miscarriages, pregnancies, and domestic violence abuse, etc. How can our young women learn to love their husbands when we as adults have set new standards and norms? Some of our young women have grown up in homes of violent abuse and they think that this is the norm. They haven't witnessed anything else. In the "Roles of the Man," we spoke on the young men seeing the same things going-on in their homes, and they also took it to be the norm. They are sadly mistaken when they grow up to become adults. Thus, we see divorces and separations on the rise. No family is exempted, because we all failed to love as God said in His Word. Love is a term we so loosely use to mean many things and not the meaning defined by God. We have media programs such as the bachelor and bachelorette wherein they're supposedly vying for one another's love, but that is not the case. Security, money, and a fling in the hay are basically what both men and women are seeking on such shows. Can we learn from these type shows? If we are faith abiding people, we can learn some pitfalls and try to avoid them.

Consequently, a wife should learn from her husband. We can debate this issue and compromise with the fact that we both husbands and wives can learn from one another. Every human being can learn from one another due to our uniqueness as individuals. Being made differently from man, there are some things a woman needs to learn from man who has the knowledge. In I Corinthians (14:34-35) Paul states:

> *"Let your women keep silence in the churches: for it is not permitted unto them to speak; but they are commanded to be under obedience, as also saith the law. And if they will learn any thing, let them ask their husbands at home: for it is a shame for women to speak in the church."*

As Paul alluded to in his discourse with the church of Corinth, there are some things that a wife might not be knowledgeable of such as church protocols, business protocols, and financial protocols. I wouldn't say that all wives are finance savvy and can conduct church operations to par. But I know they can learn if taught correctly. Because God has placed man over woman He did not endow her to master such subjects as mentioned. There was no need for the wife to learn business, finances, and church operations, because her duties were within the home. It was the husbands' duties to learn business, finances, and church operations, because God had assigned men over these entities.

On the other hand, wives are not stay-at-home moms any more. They have ventured outside of the home and have taken on tasks similar to man, thus requiring them to know the various matters. This does not make it right, but it gives the wives an outlet from the home and more ways the adversary can get us to not become children of God. I've seen wives more proficient in these matters than their spouses. And again, I have seen husbands who can not function in these matters without their wives' help. As husbands and wives, we are encouraged to help one another and to become one flesh.

God requires us to learn daily from whatever source we can see true manifestation of His Word. In order to learn His Word, we must also look at nature which can teach us dependability, trustworthiness, and volumes about God and His kingdom. According to God's Word, the inward man is renewed day by day.

CHAPTER 3

Kinds of Wives
The Disobedient Wife

The first book of the Bible gives us the first example of a wife being disobedient to her husband. In the book of Genesis (3:6-13), it states:

"And when the woman saw that the tree was good for food, and that it was pleasant to the eyes, and a tree to be desired to make one wise, she took of the fruit thereof, and did eat, and gave also unto her husband with her, and he did eat. And the eyes of them both were opened, and they knew that they were naked; and they sewed fig leaves together, and made themselves aprons. And they heard the voice of the Lord God walking in the garden in the cool of the day: and Adam and his wife hid themselves from the presence of the Lord God amongst the trees of the garden. And the Lord God called unto Adam, and said unto him, Where art thou? And he said, I heard thy voice in the garden, and I was afraid, because I was naked; and I hid myself. And he said, Who told thee that thou wast naked? Hast thou eaten of the tree, whereof I commanded thee that thou shouldest not eat? And the man said, The woman whom thou gavest to be with me, she gave me of the tree, and I did eat. And

> *the Lord God said unto the woman, What is this that thou hast done? And the woman said, The serpent beguiled me, and I did eat."*

Disobedience to God is considered outright disrespectful. God had instructed Adam and Eve of the good, the bad, and of the way of life in the garden. Yes, Eve knew this, but she still disobeyed God's instructions. Not only, did she disobeyed God, but also her husband. Through her actions and disobedience, she caused everyone born of flesh and blood to go through a regeneration process. The Adamic nature had allowed sin to come in and it had to be purged from man's nature through the blood of Jesus Christ. This sin causes us today to be atoned for by Christ.

I guess God did not make it perfectly clear that the woman must not be permitted to speak for the family, only for herself. She also is not allowed to make decisions on her own when it comes to effects on the family. We can clearly see that Eve allowed herself to be drawn in a conversation that she was not equipped to handle and to make the right decision. God had given dominance to man and expected man to govern himself accordingly to that. Adam stood idly by and allowed Eve to speak for them with the serpent which was more subtil than any beast of the field which the Lord God had made. Although Eve knew what God had said unto them, but the serpent still beguiled her into desiring and wanting the fruit of the tree. There are numerous scriptures in the Holy Bible stating that woman should not be the head, leader, or have authority over a man. She was made from man, for man.

Paul stated it very clearly in I Corinthians (11:3, 7-10):

> *"But I would have you to know that the head of every man is Christ; and the head of the woman is the man; and the head of Christ is God. For a man indeed ought not to cover his head, forasmuch as he is the image and glory of God: but the woman is the glory of the man. For the man is not of the woman; but the woman of the man. Neither was the man created for the woman; but the woman for the man. For this cause ought the woman to have power on her head because of the angels."*

Moreover, I Timothy (2:10-15) states:

> *"Let the woman learn in silence with all subjection. But I suffer not a woman to teach, nor to usurp authority over the man, but to be in silence. For Adam was first formed, then Eve. And Adam was not deceived, but the woman being deceived was in the transgression. Notwithstanding she shall be saved in childbearing, if they continue in faith and charity and holiness with sobriety."*

Now we can summarize that God did make it perfectly clear to Adam and Eve who is in charge and who speaks for the family. Our wives are quite smart, intelligent, and matured in secular knowledge, but yet they are not permitted to speak for the family or for man. God gave us as husbands to speak for the family.

Furthermore, we as husbands allowed our wives the privileges of representing and speaking for the family. I've seen many husbands who are weak in decision making and other matters, let their wives make the decision for them. Their excuses were: our wives are matured and knowledgeable of the matters, so why not let her make it. Most men don't attend church as faithfully as women and therefore, don't know what God's Word says. Genesis (3:16) says:

> *"Unto the woman he said, I will greatly multiply thy sorrow and thy conception; in sorrow thou shalt bring forth children; and thy desire shall be thy husband, <u>and he shall rule over thee."</u>*

God cursed Adam because he had hearkened unto the voice of his wife. Is this not proof enough that God wants us as men to rule our home and be in charge of our wives? I'm not advocating the Neanderthal approach, but two flesh becoming one. Wives are required to be our help mate, to help us as men fulfill our responsibilities to God and one another. Sometimes our approach from a man's point of view causes women to behave differently than expected.

Let's look at some other instances of the manner and behavioral actions of women.

The book of Hosea brings another account of a wife who was disobedient to her husband. God was teaching Hosea His prophet about

His love for Israel and how Israel was so disobedient to Him that Hosea could not quite understand it. He allowed Hosea to marry a wife of whoredom to illustrate His point. In Hosea (1:2-3), it states:

> *"The beginning of the word of the Lord by Hosea. And the Lord said to Hosea, Go, take unto thee a wife of whoredoms and children of whoredoms: for the land hath committed great whoredom, departing from the Lord. So he went and took Gomer the daughter of Diblaim; which conceived, and bare him a son."*

Gomer, after bearing Hosea three children, began to seek other lovers and deserted Hosea. In Hosea (2:5), it says:

> *"For their mother hath played the harlot: she that conceived them hath done shamefully: for she said, I will go after my lovers, that give me my bread and my water, my wool and flax, mine oil and my drink."*

She became disobedient to her husband and went back to her old ways.

In addition, Bathsheba, who was married to Uriah the Hittite, disobeyed her vows to her husband and her God, when she had a relationship with King David. The adulterous affair caused her to lose her husband and the child. Are women so vulnerable to authority that they will do anything to please? Let's analyze this situation.

In II Samuel (11:2-5), it states:

> *"And it came to pass in an eveningtide, that David arose from off his bed, and walked upon the roof of the king's house: and from the roof he saw a woman washing herself; and the woman was very beautiful to look upon. And David sent messengers, and took her; and she came in unto him, and he lay with her; for she was purified from her uncleanness: and she returned unto her house. And the woman conceived, and sent and told David, and said, I am with child."*

Because David was king, did his authority give him the right to have Bathsheba knowing that she was a married woman with a husband in his own army? Did Bathsheba yield herself, because he was king, or did they both yield due to the sinful nature in their flesh? What suppositions were running through Bathsheba's mind as she went unto the king? Did she think about her husband being punished, if she didn't have this relationship? Some who are in authority look to do certain discipline to those that are under their command, if their spouses don't comply. We have heard and seen some of this in our Armed Services during the past years. Today, there are Generals being demoted in rank for adulterous affairs while they are in command. During such adulterous affairs, a child may be conceived and brought forth into an environment that's not conducive to being reared. David could not as some do today denounce the child as not his. He saw the error of his way, and tried to rectify it by having her husband brought from the battlefield to his home in hope of him having a relationship with her before going back to the front line. This did not happen for David and he had to take a more stringent approach, and that is to have Uriah kill in battle. Uriah was killed and Bathsheba mourned his loss. Afterward, David married her as his wife. In II Samuel (11:26-27), it says:

> *"And when the wife of Uriah heard that Uriah her husband was dead, she mourned for her husband. And when the mourning was past, David sent and fetched her to his house, and she became his wife, and bare him a son. But the thing that David had done displeased the Lord."*

Therefore, David thinking that he had rectified the situation with Bathsheba and they are now married, didn't think about repentance unto God. But God has a way of getting our attention to things that are not righteous with him, if we are His children. Are we going to get away with doing wrong while we confess Him as our savior? I don't believe so. God would have one of His servant who is in the vicinity to deal with us on the sin issue, just like He did with David. In II Samuel (12:1-12), it states:

> *"And the Lord sent Nathan unto David. And he came unto him, and said unto him, There were two men in one city; the one rich, and the other poor. The rich man had exceeding many flocks and*

> *herds: But the poor man had nothing, save one little ewe lamb, which he had bought and nourished up: and it grew up together with him, and with his children; it did eat of his own meat, and drank of his own cup, and lay in his bosom, and was unto him as a daughter. And there came a traveller unto the rich man, and he spared to take of his own flock and of his own herd, to dress for the wayfaring man that was come unto him; but took the poor man's lamb, and dressed it for the man that was come to him. And David's anger was greatly kindled against the man; and he said to Nathan, As the Lord liveth, the man that hath done this thing shall surely die: And he shall restore the lamb fourfold, because he did this thing, and because he had no pity. And Nathan said to David, Thou art the man. Thus saith the Lord God of Israel, I anointed thee king over Israel, and I delivered thee out of the hand of Saul; And I gave thee thy master's house, and thy master's wives into thy bosom, and gave thee the house of Israel and of Judah; and if that had been too little, I would moreover have given unto thee such and such things. Wherefore hast thou despised the commandment of the Lord, to do evil in his sight? Thou hast killed Uriah the Hittite with the sword, and hast taken his wife to be thy wife, and hast slain him with the sword of the children of Ammon. Now therefore the sword shall never depart from thine house; because thou hast despised me, and hast taken the wife of Uriah the Hittite to be thy wife. Thus saith the Lord, Behold, I will raise up evil against thee out of thine own house, and I will take thy wives before thine eyes, and give them unto thy neighbour, and he shall lie with thy wives in the sight of this sun. For thou didst it secretly: but I will do this thing before all Israel, and before the sun.*

As a result, David received Nathan's word and took them as the Word of God. Being a man of God, David repented unto God. Once we find ourselves condemned with the wrong we have done, then we must confess and ask God's forgiveness for it, else we will continue in sin. Sin leads us unto more sin, iniquity unto iniquity, which is unto death. But righteousness leads us unto holiness and holiness unto everlasting life.

David wasn't convicted, but was condemned by the words of the man of God. He was a worshipper and a man after God's own heart, thus he wasn't convicted by the words of Nathan. When we know the word of God and have applied it to our lives, then there is no conviction, only condemnation. I believe Paul puts it so plainly in Romans (8:1) that there is therefore now no condemnation to them which are born again believers, who walk not after the flesh, but after the spirit. Conviction comes to those who are sinners, who hear the word of God and want to change their lives. David had walked after the flesh and not after God. He knew adultery was a sin and wrong in the sight of God. He confessed his wrong to the man of God, II Samuel (12:13-14),

> *"And David said unto Nathan, I have sinned against the Lord. And Nathan said unto David, The Lord also hath put away thy sin; thou shalt not die. Howbeit, because by this deed thou hast given great occasion to the enemies of the Lord to blaspheme, the child also that is born unto thee shall surely die.*

God struck the child and the child was very sick, but eventually died. David stopped his fasting and praying, comforted his wife, and had another son, one in which the Lord loved.

CHAPTER 4

Kinds of Wives
The Obedient Wife

The term obedience means submission to authority. It has caused some problems in our society between man and woman, husband and wife, parents and children, mother and daughter, father and son, and every entity that is submissive unto another. If everyone had the mind of Christ to be willing to be submissive to rule and authority, the world would be a better place to live in without fear and death. Paul said in Philippians (2:5-8),

> *"Let this mind be in you, which was also in Christ Jesus. Who being in the form of God, thought it not robbery to be equal with God: But made himself of no reputation, and made in the likeness of men: And being found in fashion as a man, he humbled himself, and became obedient unto death, even the death of the cross."*

Every since the sin in the Garden of Eden, God had made woman submissive unto man. Very few wives have this type state of mind. With all the women's right groups and organizations, we have less wives submitting unto their spouses and authority. I'm reminded what Peter wrote in his epistle to the church that our wives should be in subjection to their husbands. And if the husbands do not obey the Word, they can at least be won by the conversation (life living) of the wives. For if a wife is obedient to God, the husband will behold her chaste conversation coupled with fear. She doesn't have to appear beautifully every day with the plaiting of the hair, wearing of gold and jewelry, and putting on of apparels, but let him be won by the hidden man in her heart, in that which is not corruptible, even the ornament of a meek and quiet spirit, which God considers a great price. Peter goes on to say,

> "For *after this manner in the old time the holy women also, who trusted in God, adorned themselves, being in subjection unto their own husbands: Even as Sara obeyed Abraham, calling him lord: whose daughters ye are, as long as ye do well, and are not afraid with any amazement. (I Peter 3:5-6).*

We have had good women role models like: Sara, Ruth, Naomi, Eunice, Lois, Anna, Lydia, Phoebe, Elisabeth, Mary, Mary Magdalene, Priscilla, and many more to give us the insights in how to live with their husbands as obedient wives.

For instance, Abraham obeyed God in his daily living that Sara saw the hand of the Lord upon him and called him, "lord." None of our wives today would call us lord, because they would not see the hand of the lord in our lives like Abraham and other great patriarchs. We as men hardly go to church to learn how to walk and live like God. Yet, there are some who live for God to get the glory out of their lives. Shall we live like men of God so that our wives can say that they are pleased to live with a man who will treat her the way God would want her to be treated?

Moreover, let's look at Philip's wife. I know that the Bible doesn't say much about her. But it implies a lot about her. In Acts (21:8-9) here, we find that our brother, Paul, was on his journey back to Jerusalem, stopped by Philip's house, and was given hospitality by Philip and his wife. Philip was an evangelist of God at this point in life being exalted from one of the first seven deacons in the church of Christ. God will exalt us in due time when we have proven ourselves in his Word which Philip had done, (Acts 6). Philip and his wife had four daughters who were all virgins and in the faith such that they were prophetesses. This speaks great volume to Philip as a man of God and to his wife as a mother of God. To have reared these young women in the faith and see that they maintained their purity in the flesh, speaks extraordinarily of his wife.

Philip, first being a deacon and then exalted to an evangelist, was not home regularly to help rear his daughters and that left his wife to do the rearing. She didn't complain when Philip allowed his Christian brother, Paul, to stay at their home. Nor, did she complain when Agabus came down and stayed also. She politely made her home available to brethren of the faith and treated them like her own family. To me, she performed all the duties toward her husband as God would have wanted her to do. She showed submissiveness to Philip and his guests. She was a mother to her daughters. She demonstrated her love to her husband and guests. She was trustworthy in this inconvenience. She was a keeper at home and kept her house in order and not disarrayed. While her guests were there, she loved her daughters just the same day to day.

In addition, Priscilla, the wife of Aquila, was also a faithful and obedient wife. We hear Paul speaks of them as he found them in Rome after Claudius had commanded all Jews to depart from Rome. They (Aquila and Priscilla) were born in Pontus, but lately came from Italy. She followed her husband from Italy to Jerusalem and the thereabouts. They were one of the most successful husband and wife team that ministered in the vineyard for God. Truly, we can see her obedience to her husband, not complaining about their living arrangement, where will their refuge be, and many other questions our wives would be asking or demanding that they know. She showed humbleness and submissiveness to her husband as God required of her. She even worked with her own hands in help providing for their living. But what most important about her is that she goes in the vineyard and help spread the Gospel and/or assist in spreading the truth.

Acts (18:24-26) states,

> *"And a certain Jew named Apollos, born at Alexandria, an eloquent man, and mighty in the scriptures, came to Ephesus. This man was instructed in the way of the Lord; and being fervent in the spirit, he spake and taught diligently the things of the Lord, knowing only the baptism of John. And he began to speak boldly in the synagogue: whom when Aquila and Priscilla had heard, they took him unto them, and expounded unto him the way of God more perfectly.*

Many wives will not go to assist their husbands in the vineyard as Priscilla. But this is exactly what God is looking for in the vineyard, two flesh becoming one. She became one with his God, one with his faith, one in the same work, one in assisting others to learn the truth, and one in living what she preaches.

Apollos was mighty in the scriptures and a very eloquent speaker. But he was not all informed of the new birth that Jesus had ushered in. He still had the knowledge of what John the Baptist had preached. After hearing Apollos preached the word, Aquila and Priscilla found that he, Apollos, needed to understand the new birth more perfectly. They took him aside and expounded unto him the new birth, how a man must be born again. Priscilla wasn't bashful to comment on the scriptures to help a fellow brother to understand the way perfectly. Some of us would have said, "Better leave him alone and let him go to God for understanding and knowledge." Is this being a brother in Christ and a brother's keeper? No, allowing our brother to remain ignorant of God's word is not obeying the word of God. If the Gospel be hid, it is hid to those that are lost. Aquila and Priscilla did the righteous thing to do, inform their brother of the correct word that Jesus wanted him to preach. Apollos accepted their teaching and admonition of the word of God as it pertains to the new birth. As they departed from him, they sent word to the brethren of Achaia to receive him. When Apollos arrived in Achaia, he helped them much which had believed through grace. Acts (18:27-28) says:

> *"And when he was disposed to pass into Achaia, the brethren wrote, exhorting the disciples to receive him: who, when he was come, helped them much which had believed through grace: For he mightily convinced the Jews and that publickly, shewing by the scriptures that Jesus was Christ."*

Jesus wants all of us to become partners working side by side in the vineyard converting unbeliever to believer. My wife and I haven't gotten to this point in our lives, but we are working toward it and hope to achieve it one day. Hurray, to Priscilla and Aquila who have hit a major milestone in their life.

CHAPTER 5

Kinds of Wives The Worldly Wife

Many women in society are more prudent and careful of their status within society. Very few women will conform to the will and ways of God. Thus, we have more that will use and abuse the fashions of this world. This trend just didn't start with our generation today. It goes back to the beginning of time with Adam and Eve, Eve desiring the fruit of the tree which God told them not to eat of. The fads and fashions of the world will move most women to use them to better their beauty. The plaiting of hair with fancy hairdos and wearing of jewelry and clothing have really moved our women from being modest to being secular and proud.

In addition, we have advanced our fashions to include cosmetology. Today, we can change our appearance to be whomever or whatever we want to become, even in cloning. If we want our children to look like our favorite movie stars or persons, then we can certainly do it with the fashions and techniques of the world today.

One notorious secular woman was Jezebel, the wife of Ahab, king of Samaria. Ahab wanted the land of Naboth, the Jezreelite, who had a vineyard adjacent to the king's palace so that he can make him a garden of herbs. But Naboth would not give or sell the land to the king, because it was inheritance of his fathers. King Ahab went home and did not eat and just lay upon his bed. Jezebel inquired of his countenance and mood and was told about the land he wanted to use for his garden of herbs, but wasn't able to persuade Naboth to sell or trade it to him. She had never seen the King's spirit so sad and for him not to eat, was just wrong. Jezebel, being a worldly woman and pursuing her husband's desire, figured out a scheme to obtain the King's desire. She wrote letters in Ahab's name, sealed them with his own seal, and sent them unto the elders and nobles that were in his city, dwelling with Naboth. The elders and nobles in the city thought that the king himself sent the letters and therefore heeded their content. Consequently, they had Naboth brought to trial, found guilty, and stoned him to death. Afterward they sent Jezebel the results saying Naboth was stoned to death for failure to give the king the land. She had gotten what she wanted through forgery and lying. She immediately told the king, get up from your bed, cheer up and go take possession of the vineyard of Naboth. He is no longer living to withhold the property. It is now the property of the city which you rule over. Worldly wives loves the things of the world more than their spouses and will do whatever it takes to be satisfied with them. In this instance, Jezebel was not thinking of the pleasures of herself, but her husband. Most secular married women would go to great length to please their husbands, just as this example showed. Paul, as he wrote to the church of Corinth in I Corinthians (7:34), states:

> *"...but she that is married careth for the things of the world, how she may please her husband."*

Most married people care for the things that are of the world, and how they may please their spouses. But God would have us come together in the same faith, hope, and charity and strive to please him. Thereby having two flesh becoming one in spirit.

On the other hand, I have seen women who are quite worldly rule their homes and become rulers over the men and children. This was also a trait Jezebel demonstrated in her having Naboth stoned to death for his land. With the advent of women's liberation, women have ushered themselves to become candidates for the top office in the land. Everywhere you look women are filling the roles of men and have left the home. It's all because of the worldly lust, the lust of the eyes, and the pride of life. They seemed not to want to submit to the standards that God had set for man and woman. The roles of the man and woman must be observed if we want to have a harmonious relationship with one another and God. This is one of the many reasons our societies are in such bad conditions. Everyone is out of synch with God and His will that we have established our own will and ways. The saying is that God's ways are old fashion and we're living in modern times. Things have changed to the point that it is not profitable to live that way any longer. Some of our leaders are saying that the church must evolve or it is going to be left behind. I don't believe that. What I do believe is that if we don't seek God's will and ways we will be the most miserable people on earth, doomed and damned.

Moreover, Gomer, Hosea's wife, was another worldly woman who had her own interest at heart. She married Hosea and had his three children, but it did not stop her from pursuing her own desires. She, like many single and married women, would change to other things, but their main desires or goals are only set aside for awhile. In Hosea (1:2) states:

> *"The beginning of the word of the Lord by Hosea. And the Lord said to Hosea, Go, take unto thee a wife of whoredoms and children of whoredoms: for the land hath committed great whoredom, departing from the Lord."*

Gomer remained married unto Hosea until her desires turned toward her lovers again, and she left Hosea and went back into whoredom.

In Hosea (2:5), it states,

> *"For their mother hath played the harlot: she that conceived them hath done shamefully: for she said, I will go after my lovers, that give me my bread and my water, my wool and my flax, mine oil and my drink."*

Most secular women will put their careers and independence on hold for awhile to test marriage life out. Seeing that this is not what gives them their flare, security, and independence, they will return to the secular life they had lived before, just as Gomer. When Mr. righteous comes along and rule over her, then she will settle down and be submissive to him.

Hosea had to do this to Gomer. No doubt man has to rule his home and let the wife know that God had made him to rule over her. Most men would not let their spouses know that they rule the home and have put down some standards for the home. From Hosea and Gomer, we learned: that he had a heart to heart talk with his wife, that he had purchased her with a price, that she will abide with him many days, that she shall not play the harlot or run around with other men, and that he will be there for her. Otherwise, Gomer would not have settled down to be his wife and only his. Hosea, being told by the Lord to go and get Gomer back from the slave market and restore her as his wife without laying down some ground rules for her return would have been useless. He being obedient to God now understand what God in the beginning was trying to get him to see and understand. How often do you see husbands and wives joining the church for awhile and afterward they have gone back into the world. Some say that they have out grown the church. The church isn't keeping up with their needs. It's too old fashion. The culture isn't the same as the contemporary churches.

CHAPTER 6

Kinds of Wives
The Humble Wife

God wants each of us to be humble and meek. Whereby we find humbleness is of the flesh and meekness is of the spirit. When these traits exist within us, we will be obedient to God and one another. It is exceptional to find an obedient woman in this day and time. Nevertheless, there are humble wives in our societies. Let's not even mention the reality shows about "Housewives of ____." Humble, they are not. Yet, there are many humble wives in the Bible days.

Let's take a look at Ruth and Naomi who lived in those days when judges ruled. God had a famine to enter the land and caused many to leave Bethlehem –judah and to sojourn in the country of Moab. Elimelech, his wife, Naomi, his two sons, Mahlon and Chilion, Ephrathites of Bethlehem-judah were some who came to live in the country of Moab. They lived there until Naomi's husband died. Then her two sons married wives of the women of Moab to remain in Moab and to keep the family together. The name of the one was Orpah, and the name of the other, Ruth. They dwelt there for ten years until both Mahlon and Chilion died, leaving Naomi with her two daughters in law.

After her two sons had died, Naomi decided to return unto her own land. The famine was over and the Lord had visited his people and gave them bread. She and her two daughters in law returned unto the land of Judah. All three of the women were humble toward one another and cared for each other. They had established a bond that seems unbreakable. The two daughters in law had showed much humbleness toward Naomi that they wept over her not wanting to depart from her. In Ruth (1:8-10) it says:

> *"And Naomi said unto her two daughters in law, Go, return each to her mother's house: the Lord deal kindly with you, as ye have dealt with the dead, and with me. The Lord grant you that ye may find rest, each of you in the house of her husband. Then she kissed them; and they lifted up their voice, and wept. And they said unto her, Surely we will return with thee unto thy people."*

What humbleness, respect, and love, Ruth and Orpah showed unto Naomi. Can we find this type bond or relationship among our in-laws today? Most of the times in-laws and parents don't get along well, but this wasn't the case with Naomi, Orpah, and Ruth. The present trend is that we don't extend our families to include the in-laws just the one we marry. The brothers and sisters of the in-laws are not treated the same as the brothers and sisters of the family. You hear some rumblings that I didn't marry into their family, I only married the son or the daughter.

Because there was humility and meekness among them, they got alone very well together. Naomi humbled herself to her two daughters in law and wanted the best for them instead of letting them take care of her as she aged. Orpah decided to return to her people, but Ruth decided otherwise. You will never see more humbleness and meekness between two women like Ruth and Naomi in the Old Testament. I'm appalled at the words Ruth spoke to Naomi, as Naomi was trying to get her to return also to her people. Society doesn't recognize the fact that once we get married to another family, we accept and bond with that family like our own. Today, our societies can't bear the closeness. Not only must we as husbands and wives accept our in-laws as part of our natural family, but accept each other's faith, relatives, place of residency, and God. Now, that is what you called being humble and meek. Do we have this today? There's probably a little of this, but not to make a difference. Ruth (1:14-18) says:

"And they lifted up their voice, and wept again: and Orpah kissed her mother in law; but Ruth clave unto her. And she said, Behold, thy sister in law is gone back unto her people, and unto her gods: return thou after thy sister in law. And Ruth said, Intreat me not to leave thee, or to return from following after thee: for whither thou goest, I will go; and where thou lodgest, I will lodge: thy people shall be my people, and thy God my God: Where thou diest, will I die, and there will I be buried: the Lord do so to me, and more also, if ought but death part thee and me. When she saw that she was stedfastly minded to go with her, then she left speaking unto her."

Naomi accepted the fact that Ruth was not going to change her mind about returning to her people, so she humbled down and allowed her to stay with her.

Similarly, Mary, a virgin espoused to a man named Joseph, showed much humbleness with the angel Gabriel. God had sent him down to inform Mary of the good news, she has been highly favoured of the Lord and blessed among women. Luke (1:26-28) states:

"And in the sixth month the angel Gabriel was sent from God unto a city of Galilee, named Nazareth, To a virgin espoused to a man whose name was Joseph, of the house of David; and the virgin's name was Mary. And the angel came in unto her, and said, Hail, thou that art highly favoured, the Lord is with thee: blessed art thou among women."

With such nurturing words, Mary could do nothing else, but humble herself unto Gabriel. How would you like to be chosen by God to be the one to bring his Son into the world? This is no trivia feat. To be selected out of all the women on earth at that particular time, and designated as the mother of God's Son, it is out of mind.

Mary had lived as an unmarried woman who careth for the things of the Lord and how she may please the Lord. Her living holy in both body and in spirit really got God's heart for her to be chosen by Him. Today, our young ladies are not striving to maintain chastity due to the peer pressure and bullying which we find so prevalent in our environment. The saying among our young people now is that you're a nerd or queer if you hadn't had a sexual relationship before leaving high school. Thus, this is one of the reasons we see so many children having children just to meet the peer pressure and to be liked. Mary and other young women like her were brought up in homes with parents reverencing God. The majority of our children are not being provided with a home that acknowledges God or even talks about God. They can't go to school anymore and learn of Christ because He has been taken out of the school environment. Children who are reared in homes of God fearing parents are most likely to be obedient and humble. Children who are reared in Christian's homes are, humble, obedient, loving, and faithful with good morals and ethical standards. Such was the case with Mary. Thus, when Mary saw and heard the words of Gabriel, she was troubled and thought about what this all meant. In Luke (1:29-33), it states:

> *"And when she saw him, she was troubled at his saying, and cast in her mind what manner of salutation this should be. And the angel said unto her, Fear not, Mary: for thou hast found favour with God. And, behold, thou shalt conceive in thy womb, and bring forth a son, and shalt call his name JESUS. He shall be great, and shall be called the Son of the Highest: and the Lord God shall give unto him the throne of his father David: And he shall reign over the house of Jacob for ever; and of his kingdom there shall be no end."*

No doubt, Mary was astonished at Gabriel's saying and responded with her question – "How shall this be, seeing I know not a man?" She had kept her chastity all her youth days and still was maintaining her purity. Her up-bringing was remarkable and it speaks well of her family. There were no dating and outing with boys or outing with the girls and meeting the fellows. She didn't stay away from church, but was always in attendance with her parents. Some of our children have never seen the inside of a church, less more go to church. Moreover, in our society, our children decide whether we attend church or not. Are we going to be parents or be friends of our children? I have seen parents trying to be friends of their children and have left out structure, rules and standards of the home. I know you will say that Mary and those weren't living in a society as ours today. The same laws apply today as were yesteryears. Can God and others speak well of us?

I think not, because we are simply failing as parents. We cannot discipline our children when needed. And if we do, the department of Social Services will know and visit our homes. Our children know how to avoid being disciplined so that they can have their way. Not only are we failing in rearing our children, but we are also failing to include them in our worship services of our Lord and Saviour Jesus Christ. Getting them to reverence God as Creator and God of this world, is out of the question. This technological phase has consumed our young to believe that worshipping God must be portable or small enough that they can carry it with them. Have you ever seen the young people walking down the street with their portable devices in hands and on? Have you been in a restaurant and seen our young people at tables and counters with their hand held devices? Some were eating with the device in hand, etc. It's amazing how Satan has captivated their minds and having them to believe that God is not real.

Nevertheless, Mary was not like our young people today who seem to be transfixed with the tech world. In Luke (1:34-38), it states:

> *"Then said Mary unto the angel, How shall this be, seeing I know not a man? And the angel answered and said unto her, The Holy Ghost shall come upon thee, and the power of the Highest shall overshadow thee: therefore also that holy thing which shall be born of thee shall be called the Son of God. And, behold, thy cousin Elisabeth, she hath also conceived a son in her old age: and this is the sixth month with her, who was called barren. For with God nothing shall be impossible. And Mary said, Behold the handmaid of the Lord; be it unto me according to thy word. And the angel departed from her."*

Consequently, Mary's humbleness and meekness prevailed in this situation with Gabriel and she was delighted to be chosen as one of God's handmaids who will birth his Son into the world. While Mary rejoiced over the good news of her selection, she also remembered the angel had mentioned her cousin Elisabeth was also six month with child.

Desiring to see Elisabeth, Mary arose and entered the city of Juda. There she entered the house of Zacharias, and saluted Elisabeth. Something spectacular happened when Mary greeted Elisabeth, the baby (John the Baptist) leaped in her womb for joy. What was spectacular was the filling of Elisabeth with the Holy Ghost and also her child. Elisabeth then humbled herself to Mary as being the mother of the Lord. Luke records this conversation in (1:41-48):

> *"And it came to pass, that, when Elisabeth heard the salutation of Mary, the babe leaped in her womb; and Elisabeth was filled with the Holy Ghost: And she spake out with a loud voice, and said, Blessed art thou among women, and blessed is the fruit of thy womb. And whence is this to me, that the mother of my Lord should come to me? For, lo, as soon as the voice of thy salutation sounded in mine ears, the babe leaped in my womb for joy. And blessed is she that believed: for there shall be a performance of those things which were told her from the Lord. And Mary said, My soul doth magnify the Lord, And my spirit hath rejoiced in God my savior. For He hath regarded the low estate of his handmaiden: for behold, from henceforth all generations shall call me blessed."*

Likewise, as Ruth and Naomi showed great humbleness and meekness toward one another in the Old Testament, Mary and Elisabeth did also in the New Testament. No greater humility and meekness can be shown between two women than Elisabeth and Mary. Two women who accepted the roles which God had chosen for them to play in His plan of Salvation loved and respected each other so dearly.

CHAPTER 7

Kinds of Wives
The Prayerful Wife

As we previously stated before, everyone needs to pray to God the Father whether you're married or not. It's part of our earthly duty to God. Being married makes it even more important. Each spouse knowing his or her roles in the marriage make marriage life more enjoyable and worthy. A husband should know that he is the head of the family and should be able to lead the family in prayer at any time. God is depending on him for leadership and guidance for the family. He also should know that his wife is the weaker vessel and that God had made her that way. She is not equipped with the same muscles as him. He should honor her as his respective mate and lead her in the ways of the Lord. One of those ways is reverencing and praying to God of all creation. God requires both husband and wife to pray individually and/or collectively. To have both husband and wife praying to God in agreement, it is quite a blessing.

On the other hand, not having both husband and wife in prayer of agreement can cause delays and hindered prayer results. For as a couple, we should know that we are heirs together of the grace of life.

Today, most couples do not know that they can hinder the prayer of the other simply by not being in agreement with the spouse's desires of God. You can be asking God for a child, job, promotion, etc., and if the spouse is not in agreement with you, the prayer will not be answered. Many times, I have counseled couples and asked if they have informed each other of their prayer requests, and they will say yes and no. Yes, I was informed; no, I didn't agree for it to come to pass. Thus, the prayer is hindered, because the other spouse didn't want it to happen. The Word didn't say it will not come about, only that it will be delayed until both spouses come to an agreement.

In addition, the other way our prayers are hindered is by Satan and his forces. In the book of Daniel, Daniel said unto the Lord that they had sinned, have committed iniquity, have done wickedly, have rebelled, even departing from His precepts and from His judgments. Neither had they harkened unto His servants the prophets, which spoke in His name to our kings, princes and our fathers, and to all the people of the land. And Daniel wanted some understanding and guidance from the Lord pertaining to this and the Revelation of the Seventy Weeks. God dispatched the angel "Gabriel" to give him the skills and understanding in which he will need. But the Seventy Weeks, God dispatched another Heavenly messenger to bring the answer to Daniel, but the angel could not get through the forces of Satan who had blocked him in the heavens. Returning back to God, God dispatched Michael, one of the chief princes, along with the Heavenly messenger to deliver Daniel's prayer answer.

It took Daniel twenty-one days to receive his prayer answer due to the angel being blocked by Satan's forces. In Daniel (10:12-13), it states:

> *"Then said he unto me, Fear not, Daniel: for from the first day that thou didst set thine heart to understand, and to chasten thyself before thy God, thy words were heard, and I am come for thy words. But the prince of the kingdom of Persia withstood me one and twenty days: but, lo, Michael, one of the chief princes, came to help me; and I remained there with the kings of Persia.*

The archangel Michael fought through Satan's forces and delivered Daniel's answer after twenty-one days. So you see, Satan and his forces can hinder our prayer answers from arriving on time. Don't fear or panic, if God heard your request, He can deliver. God has archangels like Michael which can fight other spiritual beings that are not of His kingdom. Satan and his forces were kicked out of Heaven when Satan tried to exalt his will over God's. They now reside in the heaven below the throne of God. Others which had kept not their first estate, but left their own habitation, God has reserved in everlasting chains under darkness unto the judgment of the great day.

Furthermore, God has spirits locked up in the bottomless pit which John spoke about in Revelation 9:1. Thus, our prayers can be hindered by many forces in this complex world.

Let us now look at some prayerful wives who had asked and received of God. For example, Hannah, one of the wives of Elkanah, who was prayerful in her barrenness. Elkanah's other wife was named Peninnah, and she had children, but Hannah had no children. Elkanah would go out of the city yearly to worship and to sacrifice unto the Lord of hosts in Shiloh. And Hannah's adversary would provoke her sorely to make her fret, because the Lord had shut up her womb. The adversary kept during this year after year even as she went up to the house of the Lord. And Hannah would weep and not eat. One day Elkanah asked her why is she weeping and not eating. Why is her heart grieved? Is he not better than ten sons? No response was made by Hannah. So Hannah rose up after eating in Shiloh and was in bitterness of soul. Her answer was, she decided to pray to God and afterward wept much. She vowed a vow saying, if thou will look on the affliction of thine handmaid, remember me, and give unto thine handmaid a man child, then I will give him back unto You all the days of his life, and there shall no razor come upon his head. Also, in the temple was the man of God, Eli. Eli observed her praying, but was not hearing her words and that was because Hannah was praying in her heart. He supposed that she was drunk with wine and asked her how long would she be drunken. Hannah answered him, no my lord, I am a woman of a sorrowful spirit: I have drunk neither wine nor strong drink, but have poured out my soul before the Lord. Hannah went on to tell Eli, do not count her as a daughter of Belial: for out of the abundance of her complaint and grief she had spoken. Eli responded back unto her that God will grant her petition.

She left, went her way, and her countenance was no more sad. Elkanah had a relationship with Hannah and the Lord remembered her with a man child (Samuel).

This passage of scripture which was taken from the Old Testament is not true for us today. Yet, it is being used to speak of how women were prayerful during that era and how women should be today. Through the hardness of the people's heart, Moses allowed them to marry as many as they please, but Jesus came along in the New Testament and said it is not permitted today. Now we're back to one spouse until death does us apart.

Consequently, the teasing, barrenness, and bitterness were an impetus to her in remaining prayerful to the point that she made a vow unto God. Sometime our adversaries bring out the best prayers in our life.

In our society today we have many barren women who are not capable of birthing children into this world and they don't know where to turn. Some turn to doctors for help. Some turn to surrogates for help, and some to adoption agencies. And some just say forget it. I believe God made woman for man and that she is and/or will be able to produce off-springs. Otherwise, He wouldn't have told Eve outside the garden of Eden: I will greatly multiply thy sorrow and thy conception; in sorrow thou shalt bring forth children; and thy desire shall be to thy husband, and he shall rule over thee. Do our women who cannot bear children seek out God for their lack of? There may be a few who will seek God's help in time of need, but the majority will hearken to other voices. Not so with Hannah, she believed that the affliction she had can be removed by God. Satan might have put the affliction in her body, but God can remove it from the body. Just as the Hebrew boys, Shadrach, Meshach, and Abednego, said unto king Nebuchadnezzar;

> *"If it be so, our God whom we serve is able to deliver us from the burning fiery furnace, and he will deliver us out of thine hand, O king. But if not, be it known unto thee, O king, that we will not serve thy gods, nor worship the golden image which thou hast set up."*

Consequently, we must know who we worship and serve besides just going to the house of prayer. Hannah knew who she was worshipping and serving and went unto Him in prayer. Can you take your requests unto your God and get answers? One must know something of his God, howbeit, his capabilities, his power, his resources, his manifestation, etc. Our God is Omniscience, Omnipotent, Omnipresent, all wise, and a mighty God who can do all things. It is good to have an interaction with God so that you'll know that He exists and will hear and answer your calls for help. Hannah wasn't like the woman in the New Testament whereby she had a blood issue and had spent all her money on various doctors and instead of getting better she grew worse. But one day she heard of Jesus healing various people of many afflictions, diseases, and infirmities and she sought Him out for her healing. For she said, if I may touch but his clothes, I shall be whole. The prayer was not long, but brief and to the point. Now, all she had to do was put some efforts behind the words and she shall be whole. She pressed her way to Jesus and was able to touch the hem of his garment and immediately her blood issue was staunched.

On the other hand, if one lose her husband early in life like Anna, the prophetess, she can always devote her life over to Christ. Luke (2:36-37), it says that Anna was of great age and only been married to her husband for seven years before he died. She lived as a widow for fourscore and four years (84 yrs) departing not from the temple of God. Anna was a woman who loved God and served Him with fastings and prayers night and day in the temple.

Most women today would think this is cruel and unusual punishment to live alone when they're still young and beautiful. But Anna didn't think so because she was comforted by Jesus Christ. She and her husband did not have an opportunity to have children which are the heart of the family. Thus, she lived eighty-four years as a widow not having a need for companionship, or an intimate relationship. She demonstrated her steadfastness in Christ Jesus through her devotions, continual fastings, and prayers night and day. This is a good remedy for those widows who do not want to remarry.

CHAPTER 8

Kinds Of Wives
The Prudent Wife

There are some wives who are very smart and canny. And again there are some that are not so prudent. Women, who are of this caliber, often become independent and bosses of their homes. The husband does not rule the home or over her. We find an example of this in I Samuel (25:3-34). Nabal, of the house of Caleb, was a churlish and evil man. He was married to a woman of good understanding and a beautiful countenance by the name of Abigail.

One day as David was travelling in the wilderness being hungry with his men, he heard that a man by the name of Nabal was shearing his sheep and sent some men to ask him of his substances. David told the men:to greet Nabal in his name, to say to him thy liveth in properity, to thee be peace and also to thine house, and to all that thou hast. Also, inform him of his shepherds which we have with us and that they have not been hurt, neither was there ought missing unto them all the while they were in Carmel.

Moreover, I pray thee whatever cometh to thine hand unto thy servants, and to thy son David will be appreciative.

Nabal answered David's servants and said, I don't know this David, or the son of Jesse and there be many men who have broken away from their masters. You want me to give to someone I don't know, my bread, water, and flesh that I have killed for my shearers.

David's servants turned away from Nabal and came back and told David what Nabal said. His answer angered David and he gathered four hundred of his men and girded their swords and went unto Nabal. In the interim, one of Nabal's servants told Abigail, Nabal's wife, saying behold David sent messengers out of the wilderness to salute our master; and he railed on them. But the men were very good unto us and we were not hurt, neither missed we anything, as long as we were conservant with them when we were in the fields. After telling Abigail all that had happened to them and what actions David was contemplating to do, Abigail made haste and took food and wine. She fell before David on her face and said, let this inquity be upon me and accept the blessings I have brought be to thee and your men. David answered Abigail and said blessed be the Lord God of Israel, blessed be thou and blessed be thy advice which have kept me this day from coming to shed blood and avenging myself with mine own hand.

Abigail was a very smart woman in doing what she did, because David was headed to kill everyone in Nabal's land and house. She persuaded David with her offerings and herself at his mercy, that Nabal was childish in his thoughts and a man of the devil. Her prudence came to bear and won their freedom from being slaughtered.

Moreover, Lydia, a seller of purple, of the city of Thyatira, was also prudent and canny about herself with the brethren, Paul and Silas. Paul and Silas had come over in Macedonia to help them come to the faith. As they traveled to the main city, Philippi, they found certain abiding there wanting to know more of the word of Jesus Christ, especially some women. And on the Sabbath day they went down by the river side where the Word and prayer were accustomed to be made. During these services, Lydia was converted over to the Christian faith and remained with Paul and Silas as they ministered the Word of God down by the river side. Knowing that these men of God were going to be at Philippi for some time she invited them to stay with her.

In the book of Acts (16:12-15), it gives this account:

> *"And from thence to Philippi, which is the chief city of that part of Macedonia, and a colony: and we were in that city abiding certain days. And on the Sabbath we went out of the city by a river side, where prayer was wont to be made; and we sat down, and spake unto the women which resorted thither. And a certain*

> *woman named Lydia, a seller of purple, of the city of Thyatira, which worshipped God, heard us: whose heart the Lord opened, that she attended unto the things which were spoken of Paul. And when she was baptized, and her household, she besought us, saying, If ye have judged me to be faithful to the Lord, come into my house, and abide there. And she constrained us.*

She showed her prudence by getting Paul and Silas to stay with her if they believed that she was a believer in God. No doubt, Paul and Silas knew she had accepted the faith which they were ministering unto the women down by the river side; so therefore, they could not refuse her invitation. It is not morally good to enter someone home without having another brother to vouch for your innocence, or vice or versus if it's a sister to have another sister to witness one's innocence. Much rumors and gossip can erupt from homes where single individuals are living together for a brief period of time. It doesn't matter why they are staying together, rumors will be just the opposite of the true reason.

Paul and Silas probably remembered the words of the Lord in Matthew (10:11-16) which states:

> *"And into whatsoever city or town ye shall enter, enquire who in it is worthy, and there abide till ye go thence. And when ye come into an house, salute it. And if the house be worthy, let your peace come upon it: but if it be not worthy, let your peace return to you. And whosoever shall not receive you nor hear your words, when ye depart out of that house or city, shake off the dust of your feet."*

It is good not to allow people to speak evil of your good and especially if you are doing the will of God. Paul and Silas did not enter into the home of Lydia until she was a believer in Christ, and that was after Lydia had put the invitation in such a prudent way that they had to abide to acknowledge the fact they said she was a Christian and had received the faith. Although it was good for Paul and Silas in that they didn't have to buy food, pay for a place to stay, and other incidentals, it turned into a blessing for all. Lydia liked to do things for others and especially wanted to do something for the men of God.

CHAPTER 9

Kinds of Wives The Criticizing Wife

There are many women who will criticize their husbands because of this or that reason. This should not be, due to God making woman as a help meet to man. But our generation has seen fit not to believe what God has said in His Word. What does He say in His Word? In Genesis (2:18), it says:

> *"And the Lord God said, It is not good that the man should be alone; I will make him an help meet for him."*

Now, do we adhere to this truth or are we far off the truth as written? Naturally, we have made our own truth so that we can change it when we want to or make it fit the situation for us. We have had situations in life whereby our wives have sought help from civil organizations to help them to be respectful, lovable, wanted, and knowledgeable. Yes, man had abused his dominant role and caused women to rise up without God in their lives. This doesn't mean that they can do whatever they want to because of the abuse and misuse by man. God's Word is pretty clear when it comes to what He meant by an "help meet." An help meet to us today means the woman must be suitable to man in every mental, spiritual, social, and physical need. Can we get our generation and our wives to see this point without offense? Not after the women's suffrage we have seen swept this earth.

God's servant, Job, a man who had been married for years to his wife, found out during a test in his life that she was not the loving wife who he had married. Yes, we spend many years as husband and wife and still do not get to know one another, trust one another, love one another, obey one another, and support one another. Yet, we might have forgotten to get to know one another in our courtship period, but we definitely need to know one another in our marriage. God said that we, two flesh, come together as one. This is not happening in our societies today due to women's rights. When we find things going awry in our marriage, we seem to disengage and doubt our vows why we marry, or I just want to get out and be alone. In Job (2:7-10), it states:

> *"So went Satan forth from the presence of the Lord, and smote Job with sore boils from the sole of his foot unto his crown. And he took him a potsherd to scrape himself withal; and he sat down among the ashes. Then said his wife unto him, Dost thou still retain thine integrity? curse God, and die. But he said unto her, Thou speakest as one of the foolish women speaketh. What? shall we receive good at the hand of God, and shall we not receive evil? In all this did not Job sin with his lips."*

Job thought that he knew his wife faithfully, but found out differently. He, as some of us, was thinking she is praying and being consoling in his conditions with the sore boils. Not so, she was brooding over his affliction and not trusting in his God. She is definitely not being an help meet, or a devoted and obedient wife. Some of our wives marry for the better, but not for the worst. This is clearly demonstrated in all the divorces being filed and seen in our communities and nation. It's not just in the United States, but world-wide. This was not the time for Job's wife to criticize him when he is striving and fighting the affliction of the adversary. The help meet role as the healthier spouse should be comforting, encouraging, edifying, ministering good things to the ill.

On the other hand she was just the opposite that it made Job, her husband, speak words of chastisement instead of words of appreciation. Resentment builds when one spouse does nothing but criticizes the other. When we as husbands hear such words as Job's wife spoke, do we as husbands chastise or discipline our spouse like Job? If we tell our wives that they speak as one of the foolish women of the world speaks, we'll be in the doghouse for weeks and no communication for days. Women are more sensitive to words than men. Doesn't this mean we overlook the wrong and not say nothing. It is the husband's job to rule over his spouse according to the Word of God, not being a dictator, or tyrant, but as a man of God who is created in the image of God and doing the will of God.

As David was bring the ark of the Lord into the city of David, Michal, Saul's daughter, looked through her window and saw David leaping and dancing before the Lord; and she despised him in her heart. After David had made an end of offering burnt offerings and peace offerings, he blessed the people in the name of the Lord of hosts. Then David returned to bless his household and Michal came out to meet him and began criticizing the man of God. She said in II Samuel (6:20),

> *"...How glorious was the king of Israel to day, who uncovered himself to day in the eyes of the handmaids of his servants, as one of the vain fellows shamelessly uncovered himself!"*

When we have enemies whether we know them or not, our enemies will also find time to criticize you. Criticism is good if it's constructive criticism. Criticizing just to be critical of one's life or good deeds is evil. The envy one had for the other who's being criticized has grown to hatred. For Michal to criticize the king of Israel, her father's own friend, and a man of the people, she has allowed her envy to advance to hatred and she'll do anything to disgrace or criticize the king. It's the same way in our society.

Let's take a quick look at the attributes that lead from envy to murder. All of us have some envy or jealousy within us. As the envy mounts up in us, then it leads to hatred. Hatred says that I really despise you or care not for you. The more I see or associate with you, the more I want to do harm or cause you to suffer somehow. When my envy gets to this level, I'm ready to physically harm or injure you, and this turns to malice. Malice says that I will hope and/or personally see harm and danger come to you. Depending upon the degree of harm or danger, I want to inflict upon you, my envy now has led me to murder. And I'm not satisfied until this is accomplished. It looks like this:

ENVY→JEALOUSY→HATRED→MALICE→MURDER
ENVY→RAGE→MALICE
ENVY→RAGE→MURDER

This is the process which Satan will normally carry his victims through. Although he can skip some of these steps and carry you directly to murder. Have you heard of individuals getting mad and going into a rage and in this rage they do murder. And after the killing or murder, they act as if they didn't know what happened. An individual in a rage is under the influence of Satan or one of his cohorts and they will not have control of their mind or faculties. Only after Satan has gotten them to do the evil deed, will they get some control over their faculties again. This is called demon possession.

We have had many instances here in South Carolina, where demon possession has committed murder and we have labeled it mental illness. You can see it all over the world. These individuals are not ill, but sin sick and spiritually possess. No normal human being wants to believe demon or spirit possession can do these things which we call heinous, lewd, wicked, etc. The Holy Bible teaches us all about spirits, devils, and demons, and we believe not. What do we think we are battling within us, flesh and blood or principalities, powers, rulers of darkness and spiritual wickedness in high places? If you want to know more on demon possession, then read my first book on "Power of the Prayer Arsenal." It talks in depth about Satan's influence and possession.

A criticizing person can see others' wrongs, but can't see his own. Jesus called this, the blind leading the blind. Luke (6:39-42) says:

> *"And he spake a parable unto them, Can the blind lead the blind? shall they not both fall into the ditch? The disciple is not above his master; but every one that is perfect shall be as his master..."*

Jesus would rather have us to examine ourselves before trying to cleanse others. Therefore, we should not be critical of others, only self.

CHAPTER 10

Kinds of Wives The Modest Wife

Depending upon the wives' upbringing, some wives are considered shy, coy, meek, bashful, or discreet. Is this good or bad for a wife? A wife, or any woman for this matter, must have some standards, morals, and ethics about herself. There must have been some important traits, characteristics, and/or attributes which Jesus used to select Mary, the mother of Jesus. If a wife has no morals and standards about herself, then she will not be an upstanding young woman, approved by society. Mary seemed to have had this trait, modest. In Luke (1:26-33), it speaks of Mary:

> *"And in the sixth month the angel Gabriel was sent from God unto a city of Galilee, named Nazareth, To a virgin espouses to a man whose name was Joseph, of the house of David; and the virgin's name was Mary. And the angel came in unto her, and said, Hail, thou that art highly favoured, the Lord is with thee: blessed art thou among women..."*

Mary was just a normal young lady who had some extraordinary traits about herself. She showed obedience unto her parents and to God. She was taught how to carry herself and to maintain her purity and chastity. She had high standards about herself, because she was still a virgin, untouched by a young man, never kissed, not even a holding of hands. Mary understood what a virgin status meant during those days.

A man could not give his daughter(s) away unless they were virgins, or his dowry would not be worth much. Thus, Mary lived what her parents had taught her, but she also lived the commandments of God as a standard of living and setting an example for those to follow. To be spoken of as being highly favoured, speaks volume of Mary. Here is a young woman who has not been contaminated, polluted, soiled, touched, caressed, abused, or kissed by a young man. This is highly favored by God, because He wants us all to have purity of our flesh and spirit. Mary gets a hat-off to this.

Moreover, to be spoken of as the Lord is with thee, speaks to her obedience to God's Word. She has been reared in a home that nurtured and admonished her in the ways of the Lord, whereby today very few young ladies are being reared in a Christian loving home. I have no doubt that Mary's parents were God fearing people and lived the way God wanted them to live. Otherwise, Mary would not be spoken of as the Lord is with thee. Ephesians (6:1-4) states:

> *"Children, obey your parents in the Lord: for this is right. Honor thy father and mother; which is the first commandment with promise; That it may be well with thee, and thou mayest live long on the earth. And, ye fathers, provoke not your children to wrath: but bring them up in the nurture and admonition of the Lord."*

Again, Mary, being well chosen for her faithfulness, obedience, and worshipping of God, was found of God blessed among women. Her self esteem wasn't low but very high. Today our women's self esteem is waning and seems to be very low, if at all there. Reason being is that our parents didn't set high moral and ethical standards. Also, our children are not looking to have high self esteem or good morals and ethics about themselves due primarily to wanting to belong or to be a friend. Mary was the exception, she didn't look to belong or be friendly with others, her main goal in life was to satisfy her parents and God.

Similarly, there was a queen by the name of Vashti who was also modest in her living. In the book of Esther (1:9-12), it states:

> *"Also Vashti the queen made a feast for the women in the royal house which belonged to king Ahasuerus. On the seventh day,*

> *when the heart of the king was merry with wine, he commanded Mehuman, Biztha, Harbonacas, the seven chamberlains that served in the presence of Ahasuerus the king, To bring Vashti the queen before the king with the crown royal, to shew the people and the princes her beauty: for she was fair to look on. But the queen Vashti refused to come at the king's commandment by his chamberlains: therefore was king very wroth, and his anger burned in him."*

Some men marry to show off their wives such as king Ahasuerus. Being a little intoxicated with wine, he decided to show his queen off before his princes and the people. But Vashti being modest and having high self esteem didn't entertain his command. She apparently had some morals and ethics about herself that she was not going to be used as a show girl or entertainer. Many of our young women who are fair and beautiful would jump at the chance to flaunt before men and especially people of high status, not queen Vashti. Would we do our wives like king Ahasuerus did Vashti? It's a toss-up, some will and some would not even consider such an idea. As for myself, I would not parade my wife before anyone. She's my companion, lover, mother of my children, grandmother of my grandchild, and therefore I will respect her as the young beautiful wife of mine. No one should make his spouse change his or her comfort zone for entertainment for others. Because queen Vashti didn't come and show off her beauty before the king, princes, and people, she was let go as queen.

The story is very sad in context, because her spouse, king Ahasuerus, didn't respect her dignity and self esteem, only his pleasure. When one is under the influence of substances and other drugs, you don't think as clearly as you should and therefore can cause harm to come to the very one we love. The king being drunk with wine for several days was certainly not in his right mind which caused his wife to be put away. In Esther (1:12-22) it states:

> *"But the queen Vashti refused to come at the king's commandment by his chamberlains: therefore was the king very wroth, and his anger burned in him. Then the king said to the wise men, which knew the times, (for so was the king's manner toward all that*

> *knew law and judgment: And the next unto him was Carshena, Shethar, Admatha, Tarshish, Meres, Marsena, and Memucan, the seven princes of Persia and Media, which saw the king's face, and which sat the first in the kingdom;) What shall we do unto the queen Vashti according to law, because she hath..."*

As a result of a young woman trying to keep her self esteem, dignity, and modesty, she was treated as a bad influence for other women and was made an example for other women not to follow. Vashti lost her role as queen and was replaced by Esther. But to prevent the other wives and women to not disobey their husbands and princes, the king had to make a royal commandment from him and let it be written among the laws of the Persians and the Medes and that it be not altered. Vashti could no longer come before the king and her royal estate went unto another that was better than she. The royal commandment was published throughout the empire, causing the wives to give to their husbands honor, both great and small. Furthermore, the royal commandment made every man bear rule in his own house.

CHAPTER 11

Kinds of Wives The Cruel Wife

Some women are just downright cruel. Their cruelty comes from being told the truth in some instances. Others' cruelty comes from being vengeful and hateful. There are many women who have shown signs of cruelty.

For instance, Herod was told by the man of God, John, that it is not lawful for him to marry Herodias. Matthew (14:3-11) records it as follows:

> *"For Herod had laid hold on John, and bound him, and put him in prison for Herodias' sake, his brother Philip's wife. For John said unto him, It is not lawful for thee to have her. And when he would have put him to death, he feared the multitude, because they counted him as a prophet..."*

Herodias was furious over John the Baptist telling her she could not have Herod, because Philip was not yet dead. Most high society women don't believe in the spouse has to be dead in order to break the bond between her and her previous spouse. Death is the only thing that breaks the bond between husbands and wives and allows them to marry another. Both of them did not take what John said very seriously, and ended up with hatefulness and malice in their hearts. Herodias found a way to get her revenge after all. It was cruel and calculating to accomplish, but nevertheless it was done. In our passage,

Herodias knew the weaknesses of her husband, Herod, and knowing that his birthday was approaching, she could get an accomplice, her daughter to dance and get him to offer her something. She conspired with her daughter that the offer or gift would be John's head in a charger. In our day and time, we would call this cruelty at its best for her to wait on her vengefulness and use her own daughter and husband to exact it.

In addition, Pharaoh's wife showed her cruelness by lying against Joseph after his refusal to accommodate her in bed. Some women hate to be refused when it comes to their wants and desires. In Genesis (39:6-20), it says:

> *"And he left all that he had in Joseph's hand; and he knew not ought he had, save the bread which he did eat. And Joseph was a goodly person, and well favoured. And it came to pass after these things, that his master's wife cast her eyes upon Joseph; and she said, Lie with me. But he refused, and said unto his master's wife, Behold, my master..."*

Joseph knew better than to dishonor his master's house, violate his master's trust, and disobey his God by committing this sin and did the best thing, fled from his predator. By fleeing, he left his garment behind and being disappointed by Joseph's refusal, Pharaoh's wife was infuriated with Joseph and revenge was the method of repayment. She wickedly began to scheme before the lord of the house came home. The men were on her side and were not going to say anything against the master's wife, if they wanted to continue to live. When her husband came home, she immediately began to tell him how he had brought a Hebrew servant in among them and how he had tried to mock her. Upon hearing his wife's statements, the lord's wrath was kindled and threw Joseph in the prison.

As a result, Pharaoh's wife's cruelty had gotten its results. She proved that it is not customary to refuse a woman in her desires or wants. Even we as husbands can relate to this in today's world. We would find ourselves in the doghouse, or no meals, no communication for a week, no intimacy, and so on. Our nature can cause us, both men and women, to become cruel at times and the only thing that we want is revenge.

Cruelty in a marriage should not be, because we are supposed to be two flesh becoming one. Love, caring, and sharing each other should be foremost in our relationship, not striving to get back at each other.

CHAPTER 12

Kinds of Wives The Righteous Wife

Paul stated to his son in the ministry, Timothy, in II Timothy (1:5),

"When I call to remembrance the unfeigned faith that is in thee, which dwelt first in thy grandmother Lois, and thy mother Eunice; and I am persuaded that in thee also."

The righteousness of Timothy's mother and grandmother was instrumental in inspiring Timothy to live righteously. With righteous women like these, their children would have had good role models and mentors to follow after. Not to say that they will be reared in a holy home, nurtured and admonished, growing up knowing the Lord. We as parents are our children biggest role model for life. What is actually going on in the home is the normal for them. That's why it is very important that we rear them up in the Lord's faith and show them how it is lived and followed.

Apparently with Eunice and Lois, Timothy had two women in his life that really loved the Lord and wanted him to do likewise. He wasn't rebellious like some of our children today who refuse to obey parents, don't attend the house of the Lord, don't know how to pray, and live for self and friends.

Furthermore, Lydia, a seller of purple, of the city of Thyatira, was converted under the ministry of Paul by a river side. She was already striving to live righteously by joining in the prayer service with other women by the river side before Paul and Silas came along. But hearing the word of God, it converted her to Christianity and she attended to all the words which were spoken by Paul. With her conversion, she became a role model for some of the other women in that area. And because Paul's and Silas' ministry was effective, she gave them her hospitality and extended their stay in Macedonia.

Also, Priscilla, the wife of Aquila, who helped Paul in his ministry greatly, was another wife whose work in the Lord was vividly seen in the work along with her husband, Aquila. She even allowed a church to be assembled in her home and did service unto those that attended. Paul spoke very highly of her and the church which was in her home. In Romans (16:3-5), it states:

> *"Greet Priscilla and Aquila my helpers in Christ Jesus: Who have for my life laid down their own necks: unto whom not only I give thanks, but also all the churches of the Gentiles. Likewise greet the church that is in..."*

Moreover, Paul had come down to Corinth and there at Corinth, he met Aquila and Priscilla who had departed from Rome due to Claudius commanding the Jews to depart from Rome. He, Paul, came unto them because they were also of the same craft, and abode with them, wrought with them for by their occupation they were tentmakers.

In addition, Anna, a prophetess, the daughter of Phanuel, of the tribe of Aser, was also a righteous wife and was spoken of by Luke. In Luke (2:37-38), it says:

> *"And she was a widow of about fourscore and four years, which departed not from the temple, but served God with fastings and prayers night and day. And she coming in that instant gave thanks likewise unto the Lord, and spake of him to all them that looked for redemption in Jerusalem."*

Anna had lived with her husband for seven years before he was deceased. She never married again due to her devotion to God and her work in the ministry. She maintained her steadfastness in the Lord after her husband died and overcame the lusts and desires of the flesh.

This speaks very highly of her faith as Paul had written to Timothy in I Timothy (5:3-14):

> *"Honour widows that are widows indeed. But if any widow have children or nephews, let them learn first to shew piety at home, and to requite their parents: for that is good and acceptable before God. Now she that is a widow indeed, and desolate, trusteth in God, and continueth in supplications and prayers night…"*

It is obvious that Anna had been taken into the number of widows by the church under the age of threescore years.

She had only lived with her husband for seven years, and she had been a widow of fourscore and four years. She didn't allow her flesh to wax wanton as Paul stated most young widow would have done. She definitely did not cast off her first faith and learn how to be idle, like some of our young widows do today. Anna served God with fastings and prayers night and day in the temple. She totally dedicated herself unto the Lord and diligently followed every good work. Being such an aged one, she no doubt had washed the feet of some of the saints; she had relieved the afflicted; and she had lodged strangers. These things the church looks for in widows indeed before taking them into the fold and seeing after their needs.

Another righteous wife is Elisabeth, the daughter of Aaron and the wife of Zacharias. Luke speaks of her righteousness in Luke (1:5-7):

> *"There was in the days of Herod, the king of Judaea, a certain priest named Zacharias, of the course of Abia: and his wife was of the daughters of Aaron, and her name was Elisabeth. And they were both righteous before God, walking in all the commandments and ordinances of the Lord blameless. And they had no child, because that Elisabeth was barren, and they both were now well stricken in years."*

In this passage of scripture, we see that both the husband and wife are righteous, following the Lord's commandments.

This is just what God wants us to do as husbands and wives. Zacharias being a priest and exercising the priest's office speak volume of the man of God. Not only is he taking care of the office of the Lord, but insuring that his family is abiding by God's commandments also. The husband is the one in the home who is supposed to be the leading figure as lordship, mentor, and disciplinarian. Although he can delegate his disciplined role to the wife, if need be.

Again, here are two flesh which has become one. The scripture says that they both were righteous, walking in all the commandments, and ordinances of the Lord blamelessly. That's a goal we as husbands and wives must set for our marriages when we both become believers of God and His Word. God expects a lot out of us as leaders of his people, and rewards us accordingly. Here, he rewarded Zacharias and Elisabeth with a child who will become the forerunner of His Son, Jesus Christ. Yet, her womb was barren, well stricken in age, God rewarded them with a son. Many women today who are barren give up hope of ever becoming fruitful unto their husbands. Not if you are a child of God, because all things are possible with God. With our doctors, we will find this impossible. I believe that God made all women to be able to bear children.

Furthermore, since this child was going to be the forerunner of His Son, Jesus Christ, Elisabeth had to be made holy also. An emcee that is impure cannot pronounce the coming of someone that is pure without going through a purification process like God did with Elisabeth. Luke (1:41) states:

> *"And it came to pass, that, when Elisbeth heard the saluation of Mary, the babe leaped in her womb; and Elisabeth was filled with the Holy Ghost:"*

Since John needed to be holy, Elisabeth was also made holy. Now, we can understand why she was filled. John being in his mother's womb is a part of her, and therefore was also made holy. Now he is capable and has all qualifications to be the forerunner of Jesus Christ.

CHAPTER 13

Kinds of Wives The Lying Wife

No man wants a woman that is untruthful, especially if she is a lying individual. For we had talked about Pharoah's wife as she lied upon Joseph due to his refusal of her advances which caused him to be bound in Pharoah's prison. Another is Gomer, the wife of Hosea, who lied to her husband that she will give up her fornication and be his wife, but eventually she went back to her old ways.

Moreover, Delilah lied to Samson to get him to reveal his strength and power so that she can betray him into the hands of the Phillistines.

Furthermore, Sapphira lied to Peter about the money she and her husband received for the possession they sold. They were supposed to give all the proceeds to the church to help alleviate the poverty in and around Jerusalem, but they decided to keep back part for themselves. Her husband was struck down by God without her knowledge. The church men carried him out and buried him. Sapphira came later into the church unto Peter and Peter asked her, did you sell the land for so much? She replied back to Peter in the affirmative, yes, for so much. Acts (5:8-10) records the consequences of her lie:

> *"And Peter answered unto her, Tell me whether ye sold the land for so much? And she said, Yea, for so much.*

> *Then Peter said unto her, How is it that ye have agreed together to tempt the Spirit of the Lord? Behold, the feet of them which have buried ..."*

Consequently, Sapphira didn't believe that she was lying against the Holy Ghost which she had received and was dwelling within her mortal body. A wife that was in the church of the living God, under good leadership, and had the Word ministered unto her. She somehow lost her focus on Christ and began to put her affection on things on the earth. She still was believing she was saved and still filled with the Holy Ghost. Most people believe once saved and filled with the Holy Ghost, He'll never leave you. Not true! Matthew (12:31-32) says:

> *"Wherefore I say unto you, All manner of sin and blasphemy shall be forgiven unto men: but the blasphemy against the Holy Ghost shall not be forgiven unto men. And whosoever speaketh a word against the Son of man, it shall be forgiven him: but whosoever speaketh against the Holy Ghost, it shall not be forgiven him, neither in this world, neither in the world to come."*

We can sin against Jesus and it shall be forgiven us, but to sin against the Holy Ghost which makes us Holy, it is not forgiven. It doesn't matter how much we cry unto God, you will not get forgiveness, neither in this world which we live in today and neither the new world which Jesus will create for us as believers to live in with him. That is why we must be very careful when we're in the midst of sinners and talking about the Holy Ghost, because they can easily speak against Him since they do not know Him. We as believers, disciples, Christians, and saints should know Him because we had accepted Him in the process of salvation. No one can be saved without accepting the Spirit of Christ. The new birth means nothing to mankind anymore, it's shake the minister's hand and repeat the sinner's prayer after him and you're saved. This is the biggest lie ever told to man. These certain ministers tell us this because it's all they know and were told.

Nevertheless, Sapphira was not a believer anymore when she spoke against the Holy Ghost. She had sinned prior to her interaction with Peter. She conspired with her husband to defraud the church out of the money which is a sin. Her thoughts were evil and defiled her body, another sin. She had envy or jealousy against Joses who having land, sold it, and brought the money, and laid it at the apostles' feet. They tried to deceive the church and the man of God with only giving a portion of the money they received for the selling of their land, another sin. She was a partaker in her husband's sins as a wife who had agreed together. All these sins were committed by Sapphira before she came to Peter who was used by God to get her to repent and ask for forgiveness, but she refused to do so, and therefore God struck her dead within the church. She was no longer a saved individual and in the church, but was lost due to the Spirit leaving her mortal body because of unconfessed sin in her life. God will always give us an opportunity to confess our sins and ask for forgiveness, but we believe we're okay. In the book of James (5:16), it says,

> *"Confess your faults one to another, and pray one for another, that ye may be healed. The effectual fervent prayer of a righteous man availeth much."*

Sapphira was sin sick and needed to confess her faults before Peter, the man of God, so that she can be healed, not that she had a sickness upon her, but that she may be healed of the sins which she had committed and allow God to give her a refreshing of His Spirit, which He would have if she had confessed. Since she didn't, God struck her dead within the church for her speaking against His Spirit. To blaspheme against the Holy Ghost can only be done by sinners, not believers of Jesus Christ. The sad thing about this situation is that Sapphira didn't even know when the Spirit had left her. We have heard of the scripture whereby it says that God does not dwell in an unclean temple. When Sapphira did her wrongs, she had contaminated the body again and made it unclean. Therefore, the Holy Ghost had no choice but to leave her in her sins and go back unto God. And when you have not the Spirit of Christ, you are none of His. It is the Holy Ghost which gives us the link with Christ. He does a lot in the believers' life that we are not aware of. If you should be asked do you have the Holy Ghost, most people would respond, why do I need the

Holy Ghost? I will list some of the reasons why you need the Holy Ghost in today's environment:

You need Him:

- ✓ To be born again
- ✓ To quicken your mortal body
- ✓ To be adopted by Christ and the Father
- ✓ To teach believers
- ✓ To execute God's Word
- ✓ To work wonders and miracles
- ✓ To heal people
- ✓ To deliver people
- ✓ To witness and have power
- ✓ To confirm you as a child of God
- ✓ To try other spirits
- ✓ To help pray by intercessions
- ✓ To comfort you
- ✓ To reprove the world of sin
- ✓ To reprove the world of righteousness
- ✓ To reprove the world of judgment
- ✓ To show you things
- ✓ To speak in other languages
- ✓ To discern spirits
- ✓ To cultivate the hearts into singleness
- ✓ To transport one in the spirit
- ✓ To lead the children of God
- ✓ To give spiritual gifts
- ✓ To produce spiritual fruit
- ✓ To have eternal life
- ✓ To live after the Spirit
- ✓ To develop God's relationship with man
- ✓ To mortify the deeds of the body
- ✓ To make heirs of God and Christ
- ✓ To teach you how to love one another
- ✓ To anoint the garments or items
- ✓ To transform our bodies into matter

- ✓ To test our works of what sort they are
- ✓ To have abundant life in the Spirit
- ✓ To bring things back to remembrance

The Bible speaks volume of reasons why one will need the Holy Ghost. Just think, how can I live holy on this earth with my conscience just saying I'm holy? God requires more than your conscience saying you're holy. God, Himself, must make us Holy, and He does this through His giving of His Spirit unto man. It is His Spirit which makes us Holy and gives us eternal life while we are living here on earth. All we have to do is maintain Him within these mortal bodies until Christ or even death takes us out of this world. Isn't this simple enough to do?

Moreover, it's the Spirit which gives us eternal life which is also salvation. When we were naturally born into this world, we were without the Spirit of Christ who died to save us from our sins. When we are born again, we received his Spirit, are saved, and have eternal life all through a process called, the new birth. The new birth consists of water baptism and the Holy Ghost baptism. The two prerequisites, we need to have in order to be saved and have eternal life while living in this flesh.

CHAPTER 14

Kinds of Wives
The Unfaithful Wife

We have already mentioned some of the spouses' who were unfaithful to their husbands, such as Gomer, Pharaoh's wife, Herodias, and Sapphira. But Job's wife was also unfaithful in that she did not believe wholeheartedly in the same God as Job. This will make her unfaithful to the God which Job worshiped. God had male and female to come together as one. His Word says we as males and females should become one in the flesh and spirit. When we have a division of worshipping and serving God in two different faiths, then we are unfaithful to one another and God. We have many husbands and wives serving and worshipping God in their own way. One might be a Baptist and the other might be a Methodist and worship and/or serve the Lord God in two different sanctuaries. It matters to God what faith we are following in the family, because the family should all worship and serve the same faith the husband chooses. The responsibility of worshipping and serving the Almighty God belongs to the man of the house. This man of the house should know about God to the point that when he is of age, he can guide his family in the right faith. I was reared in a home similar to this. My parents were of different faiths and worshipped in different sanctuaries. As a child, I wanted to attend the Methodist church most of the time, because they turned out earlier than my father's church. But I would occasionally visit his church when my mother said to go.

After being brought up this way serving God via the Methodist and Baptist ways, I decided in my heart when I got married that my wife and I would not be split in worshipping and serving God. We'll worship in the same faith. My wife grew up as a Baptist and I grew up as a Methodist and Baptist to say. But at marriage we both decided to worship in the same faith, Baptist till I learned differently. Deep down I believed that there was a more perfect way better than the Baptist and Methodist faiths. And that faith was the Christian faith based on the Apostles' teaching and doctrine. Some people wanted to call the Christian faith, "Holiness." But I still believed that it's more than the "Holiness Way." As I studied the Word of God, it did not mention the Baptist, Methodist, or Holiness ways, only the Apostles' way which became known as the Apostolic Way. The Apostles were taught by Jesus, Himself, and they carried out His teachings and ways after He was caught up to Heaven. The four writings of the Gospel were what Jesus taught them and they diligently carried them out through the writings found in the Book of Acts and other epistles. Jesus brought us a new and living way that the Baptist, Methodist, Catholics, Muslims, Holiness, and all the other traditional ways can't align. Although most of them were taken from the Word of God, they did not align entirely to the Word of God or the Gospel of Jesus Christ. To be known as the Christian Way, the other faiths must produce the same results as the Apostles. They haven't produced any evidence like the Apostles' doctrine in my view, therefore, they are not of the Christian faith. Jesus said that there is only one way, one faith, one Lord and that's all via Him.

Lastly, Bathsheba was found to be unfaithful to her husband, Uriah, when she had an affair with King David. Her husband being out on the front line of battle for the king and she being left all alone, Bathsheba yielded to temptation. I guess the condition was just right for her to be unfaithful to her husband. Let's look at the conditions and see whether we can visualize these conditions today and can they cause a wife to be unfaithful.

Firstly, she was left all alone at home for some period of time. Secondly, she was lonely and didn't know when her husband will be back if he does come back from battle. Thirdly, she loved her beauty and wanted to feel wanted by a man. She could have loved status and people of status which the king presented. She may have seen no harm in having an affair while her husband was away, since he'll never know. She wasn't a true believer of her faith if she had faith in God, because she didn't maintain her vows to Uriah or God. She may have been caught in a weak moment, and easily seduced or she didn't care about her wifely status. Her husband could have neglected her body for a period of time and she wanted to feel like a woman who is able to satisfy a man or to be satisfied.

Regardless, Bathsheba was unfaithful to her husband and God. When lustful conditions come upon an individual he or she will try to satisfy the urges. The more you allow lust to reign in your mortal flesh, the more it will yearn in your flesh.

CHAPTER 15

Roles of the Woman

Woman – a female human being. Also defined as a girl grown up. In Genesis (2: 21-23), it states:

> *"And the Lord God caused a deep sleep to fall upon Adam, and he slept: and he took one of his ribs, and closed up the flesh instead thereof; And the rib, which the Lord God had taken from man, made he a woman, and brought her unto the man. And Adam said, This is now bone of my bones, and flesh of my flesh: she shall be called Woman, because she was taken out of Man."*

God had seen fit that man should not be alone, but made him an help meet, called woman, to keep him company and to help assist in other tasks of the garden. Woman's main task was to see to the procurement of food for the two of them. And because she was the procurer, the serpent came directly to her and started his deception. The woman, knowing where she was supposed to gather food and where she was not allowed to gather food, engaged in the conversation with the serpent. The serpent, being more subtle than any beast of the field which the Lord God had made, said unto the woman, hath God said you shall not eat of every tree in the garden. The woman replied back in the affirmative, we may eat of the fruit of the trees of the garden, but the fruit of the tree which is in the midst of the garden is not to be eaten or touched, lest we die. The serpent replied back to the woman, you shall not surely die. For God knows that in the day you eat thereof, then your eyes shall be opened and you shall be as gods, knowing good and evil. The devil does not tempt us with something we don't know, but with the things we know. He has a way with words and can cause man to bite at the temptation, just as he did with the woman. And when the woman saw that the tree was good for food and that it was pleasant to the eyes, and a tree to be desired to make one wise, she took of the fruit thereof, and did eat, and gave also unto her husband with her and he did eat.

Most women today have a special place they will procure food from because of their specificity of the food plus other things. Again, most women will buy food based on looks, color, ripeness, quantity, place of business, friends, taste after cooking, and on and on. Once the food is purchased, the woman has the task of preparing it for consumption by the number in the family. She will also taste the food before serving it out to the man, or spouse, or family. If the food is not delicious on its own merits, then the woman would add other ingredients to aid in the taste.

All women do these tasks today and I guess it was instilled in woman to do. You have to remember that Adam and Eve did not grow up from children, they were made grown up like everything else around them.

Nevertheless, the woman sinned when she gave heed to the serpent's words and did as God said not to do. In this scenario, the woman spoke out of term whereby the man should be the one making the decisions when it comes to the family or what God has said. A woman is not to make decisions when she has a man in the midst. The man sinned when he harkened unto the voice of the woman, and did eat of the tree which God said not to eat. From this time forward, woman was multiplied with sorrow and in her sorrow she shall bring forth children, and her desire shall be to her husband, and he shall rule over her. Most men and women don't attend worship services or read their Bibles to see what is required of them by God. To say the least, some don't believe in God.

In spite of what God said, woman has thrown this commandment out of mind and heart, and has replaced it with, woman is equal with man and/or better than man. A woman sees herself not a slave to man as to say. She is free to make choices and decisions on her own. She looks at things differently than a man. These instilled attributes that God gave unto woman make her unique from man, although she was taken from man. And the two of them with different attributes, qualities, and characters, make them a well rounded couple.

CHAPTER 16

Roles of the Wife

WIFE - a woman who has married a man as her husband.

When God made Eve from the rib of Adam and brought her to Adam, she became his wife. Thereafter, God said,

> *"Therefore shall a man leave his father and his mother, and shall cleave unto his wife: and they shall be one flesh."* (Genesis 2:24)

Since God has given man the dominion over all things and a ruler over his wife, leadership has been declared by God. We as husband and wife should not have any squabbles about who's the boss or the man of the house. God has even made the protocol very simple. If a man desire to have a wife, he must leave his father and mother and go find the one he wants to live with. Man has not accepted this protocol by which he must obtain his spouse. I can recall as a young man when man would ask the parents of his girl-friend for her hand in marriage. This is outdated today and much has changed with our younger generation. Before a man shall cleave unto his wife, he must have a job so that he can care for her.

This is not a requirement today, because our young people are so in love that a job has nothing to do with their well-being. It has a lot to do with their well-being and livelihood. Some of the old school parents would tell the young man, he cannot have their daughter's hand until he gets a job. Where is this stance today? It is very needful today. We as grandparents are rearing our grandchildren while our children are playing house. We have missed God's way of marriage and have gone about and established our own ways of marriage.

The wife's new roles should be framed from her mother's role while she was a child in the home. Her mother should have been a role model for her to be able to adapt to her new roles and environment. What roles did she see her mother doing in the home while her father was away working to make a living for the family? One was how the wife was taking care of the home. Another was how she planned the meals and prepared them for the husband: next how she spent time with the babies; how she blended in her personal time and time with God; and lastly when her husband came home she had time for him also. With the new advent of women's liberation and women's rights, wives have not the time to do their wifely duties anymore.

As I looked back over my childhood days when I was just a boy, I noticed how my mother work within the home while my father worked outside the home. She was always doing something in the house. If it weren't cleaning, cooking or helping us with our homework, it was washing and ironing the clothes, etc., but never outside of the home. My dad had to work two to three jobs in order to make ends meet. These roles stuck with me throughout life and they align with God's Word.

Moreover, let every wife have her own husband and let every husband have his own wife. This is one of God's principles of marriage and some religions will say other- wise. Jesus had to deal with this same issue when he was on earth with the Pharisees. Moses had to allow the people to divorce and marry and remarry, because they could not get along with each other and their hearts were hardened.

God commands the wife not to depart from her husband. But and if she depart, let her remain unmarried, or be reconciled to her husband: and let not the husband put away his wife. Do we adhere to the Word of God or do we adhere to man's philosophy? If you can't live with them, divorce them and get someone you can live with. God wants us to be happy. Right? Wrong! God has given us the choice to marry whom we will on our personal will. But when it comes to being a believer of His Word, we must adhere to it. The wife is bound by law and God to her husband as long as he liveth; but if he depart this life, then she is free to marry again, only to marry another believer in the faith of God.

Paul puts it very plainly in I Corinthians (7:10-16, 34, 39):

> *"And unto the married I command, yet not I, but the Lord, Let not the wife depart from her husband: But and if she depart, let her remain unmarried, or be reconciled to her husband: and let not the husband put away his wife. But to the rest speak I, not the Lord, If any brother hath a wife that believeth not, and she be pleased to dwell with him, let him not put her away. And the woman..."*

> *"There is difference also between a wife and a virgin. The unmarried woman careth for the things of the Lord, that she may be holy both in body and in spirit: but she that is married careth for the things of the world, how she may please her husband."*

> *"The wife is bound by the law as long as her husband liveth; but if her husband be dead, she is at liberty to be married to whom she will; only in the Lord."*

Matthew (5:31-32) states:

> *"It hath been said, Whosoever shall put away his wife, let him give her a writing of divorcement:*

> *But I say unto you, That whosoever shall put away his wife, saving for the cause of fornication, causeth her..."*

In our society today, we see that husbands and wives are constantly separating and divorcing each other for the slightest things. It's not so much the man's fault, but the woman's fault. A wife looks for a husband to please her materially more so than spiritually and physically. She has also looked for things that are pleasing to her eyes. If you can recall what Eve did in the garden of Eden, when the serpent tempted her with the fruit of the tree.

> *"And when the woman saw that the tree was good for food, and that it was pleasing to the eyes, and a tree to be desired to make*

one wise, she took of the fruit thereof, and did eat, and gave also unto her husband with her; and he did eat." Genesis (3:6)

This event lets us know that a woman looks for things that will please her more than just having a husband. Thus, this trait in woman was passed down from Eve to every wife today. This "pleasing trait" is very hard to overcome. How many times we as husbands have tried to please our spouses with material things and they cried, "That is not what I want!" Howbeit the color, style, length, or name brand. As long as it meets her approval and the husband is in agreement for her to get it, she is pleased. Have you heard of husbands sending their wives on shopping trips just to satisfy them? I know you have. It is real today. I'm not insinuating that we as husbands do this, but our wives are looking for this more and more these days. Do you hear it around the house? How did you like the meal? How do I look with this outfit? Which one should I wear? What restaurant are you taking me to? The list can go on and on. Wives like to be pleased to satisfy this trait that Eve gave unto them. Therefore, since they are so hard to please, many will divorce their husbands after a few years. Since we know this is a problem, how can we as husbands overcome this? We definitely will need God's help in this matter. What I have drawn from the scriptures and those husbands and wives in the Bible days is that God's love must be in us in order to overcome the "pleasing trait." I didn't read or see any place where they were trying to please one another as mentioned above. But I did read where they were mutually agreeable with one another: they rendered due benevolence unto one another; wives accepted their places in the home and demonstrated submissiveness unto their husbands; they accepted the husbands' faith and worshipped alongside them. As their love grew toward God, it also grew toward one another.

Let's look at some examples of how the husband and wife have overcome the trait or didn't allow the trait to interfere in the marriage. First of all, Abraham and Sarai, husband and wife, God called Abraham to leave his country, his kindred, his father's house, unto a land that He will show him. Abraham departed and took with him Lot and his wife, Sarai, unto the land that God will show him. Sarai, his wife, didn't argue with Abraham when he told her to come let's leave our relatives and go into a foreign land where we don't know what's there. Sarai didn't argue about whether God had called Abram or not. Sarai didn't say let me worship my God my way, but accepted Abraham's God and faith and lived accordingly. She didn't question Abraham about what was happening from day to day. She accepted his leadership and faith in God that there was nothing to question. She just showed submissiveness and benevolence to Abraham. Even though Abraham allowed her to be taken into Pharaoh's house as his sister, he trusted in God to work it out for their good. And the Lord did work it out for their good, by allowing plagues to come unto Pharaoh and his house because of Sarai, Abram's wife. The "pleasing trait" did not come into play in their marriage.

Mary, the mother of Jesus, and Joseph were engaged and eventually married. As husband and wife, they worshipped the same God and had the same faith. Mary had faith, trust, and confidence in her husband who will do the right thing. This is lacking in our marriages today, but was a very important fact in our fore fathers' marriages. Mary just up and went with Joseph when God sent him away to Egypt and remained there until God told him to return to Israel. Did Mary grumble about moving or question Joseph as he did what he did? No. She had love for her husband and had faith in him. Mary's and Joseph's marriage was not a quick cross the border and get married, but had a courtship period that allowed them to get to know one another. This is lacking in our society today. Their relationship cultivated trust, love, and faith in God and themselves. Love worketh no ills toward one another.

Peter and his wife, also believers in God, had the same faith, worshipped together with other believers of their faith, and were given to hospitality. She didn't mind Peter bringing Jesus and his disciples into the home for sheltering and food. She also allowed her mother to come and be in the home at times. Matthew (8:14-15) says:

> *"And when Jesus was come into Peter's house, he saw his wife's mother laid, and sick of a fever. And he touched her hand, and the fever left her: and she arose, and ministered unto them."*

Elisabeth and Zacharias, mother and father of John the Baptist, believers of the same God and worship in the same faith, loved, trusted, and respected one another. They gave no place to the "pleasing trait" as some couples might do. It could have easily come in when Elisabeth was ready to deliver John the Baptist, but their love and trust in each other overcame it. Luke (1:57-63) states:

> *"Now Elisabeth's full time came that she should be delivered; and she brought forth a son. And her neighbours and her cousins heard how the Lord had shewed great mercy upon her; and they rejoiced with her. And it came to pass, that on the eighth day they came to circumcise the child; and they called him Zacharias, after the name..."*

Elisabeth could have called his name what she wanted to name him or what her neighbors called him, but she remembered what her husband and the angel had said that he will be called. She did not hesitate to believe the angel and her husband and called his name John. Zacharias could have named him differently from Elisabeth, but both being believers of the same God and having faith in the same, called his name John, also. Their relationship, love, and trust in God overcame any I like my name verses that name. Love can remove all doubts.

Husbands and wives should be a confirmation to each other when it comes to important issues of the home as mentioned above. The wife should be able to understand her husband's position on matters and be subject unto him. Things that can affect their relationship with each other and God should be talked over before a concrete decision is made and that's by the husband because he's supposed to have more of God's Word than the wife. This is not all true today, because we have more wives more knowledgeable of God's Word than the husbands. Either way we as husbands and wives should be able to talk issues out before quickly making a decision. Each other's input is important, regardless how small it may seem. As a society, we have established our own marriage ideas, who runs the house, and who makes the decisions. We only throw God's way in our conservation when it is convenience.

Let's look at Ananias and Sapphira, husband and wife, believers of God, members of the Church of Christ. Ananias and Sapphira sold a possession of theirs to be like some of the other members of the church. But Ananias didn't want to be totally like the other members because he wanted to keep a certain portion of the money for himself. Therefore, he got Sapphira to agree that they would only give a certain portion of the money to Peter and the disciples. Sapphira agreed and confirmed Ananias' wrong doing instead of speaking against it. This is what husband and wife ought not to do when confirming one another as believers in Christ. One should not uphold another in wrong doing, but rebuke and instruct in the right way of doing things. I guess you might say that Sapphira had that "pleasing trait."

Also, Philip and his wife, a couple who was given to hospitality, used their home as a boarding house for some of the brethren. His wife was in agreement with him allowing the brethren when they were passing through their way to come in and rest as they pursue their journey. No doubt, she had to wash, cook, and feed them as they abided in their home without saying a mumbling word. Wives today would not be so eager to allow visitors to come in and be treated with royalty. But Philip and his wife were in agreement to allow other brethren to stay over as they traveled through Caesarea. With their four daughters around the house, they easily took care of the brethren, such as Paul and his companion, and Agabus.

His wife did not question him as he attended to the Lord's business like some wives do their husbands today. Philip, an evangelist, was on the go quite often and for some days. For example, his trip down to Samaria where he preached Christ unto the people, Acts (8:5-13), Acts (8:26-38), and Acts (8:39-40). His wife did not complain about him going all the time or why can't he stay home some time? They respected and trusted one another as husband and wife. Their relationship with God was matured enough that each one can be without the other for a period of time before the marriage begins to break apart. When it comes to God's way of living, we as husbands and wives must be living proof that God will keep us from breaking asunder. Yes, we will have little spats, but not to the point of separating and divorcing, if we have faith and trust in God. Being away from each other as husbands and wives can cause great consternation on a marriage.

CHAPTER 17

Roles of the Mother

Mother - A wife who has birthed a child or children into this world.

The increase in women's roles was dictated to Eve in the Garden of Eden after the downfall of man due to sin. Thereafter, God cursed the earth, man, woman, and the serpent. But unto the woman He said,

> *"I will greatly multiply thy sorrow and thy conception; in sorrow thou shalt bring forth children; and thy desire shall be to thy husband, and he shall rule over thee." (Genesis 3:16)*

This saying signified the mother's role which Eve had not had an opportunity to live until God threw them out of the garden. Inside the Garden of Eden, Adam and Eve lived as husband and wife, but outside the garden Eve and Adam lived as mother and father. Meaning they had matured to another level of living which God had eventually wanted them to achieve. Genesis (4:1-2) says,

> *"And Adam knew Eve his wife; and she conceived, and bare Cain, and said, I have gotten a man from the Lord. And she again bare his brother Abel. And Abel was a keeper of sheep, but Cain was a tiller of the ground."*

All women are expected by God to become mothers.

"And God blessed them, and God said unto them, Be fruitful, and multiply, and replenish the earth, and subdue it: and have dominion over the fish of the sea, and over the fowl of the air, and over every living thing that moveth upon the earth." Genesis (1:28)

In this verse God had blessed "woman" to replenish the earth. It didn't say that some women will and there be those who cannot replenish. Does God expect all women to be fruitful and replenish the earth? I believe He does. Let's look at Abraham and Sarai, husband and wife, who were not immediately able to bear a child. Genesis (11:29-30) states,

"And Abram and Nahor took them wives: the name of Abram's wife was Sarai; and the name of Nahor's wife, Milcah, the daughter of Haran, the father of Milcah and the father of Iscah. But Sarai was barren; she had no child."

Sarai was not able to have a child, but yet God promised Abram a child in his marriage. If God promised Abram a child from his wife to be the seed, then God will insure it happens. With God if He promise, then it will come to past.

Genesis (21:1-3) states,

"And the Lord visited Sarah as he had said, and the Lord did unto Sarah as he had spoken. For Sarah conceived and bare Abraham a son…"

God had to bless Sarah's womb to be fruitful so that his saying to Eve, mother of the women, can be fulfilled. Barren or not God expects all women's womb to be fruitful and bring forth children. Some of our women might say otherwise because they are not able to have a child. As Sarah found out with God, all things are possible. We have not because we ask not. Sarah eventually became a mother just as God wanted her to become. This saying is intended for all women regardless of their wombs' status or marital status.

Moreover, there was another couple who were married and could not have a child. Yet they were both righteous before God, walking in all the commandments and ordinances of the Lord blamelessly. They had no child because his wife was barren. Luke (1:5-7) states:

> *There was in the days of Herod, the king of Judaea, a certain priest named Zacharias, of the course of Abia: and his wife was of the daughters of Aaron, and her name was Elisabeth..."*

When we as husbands and wives live according to God's commandments, God will bless our coming and going. This is to let us know that all things are possible with God. There's nothing too hard for God, plus He blesses us with those things we need in order to fulfill our roles and destiny. Zacharias, knowing his wife was barren and not able to have children, prayed to God for her to have a child. This is the remedy for all wives who cannot have a child because they are barren. But we don't hear of husbands and wives praying to God for a child in situations like this. The majority of the time the spouses will visit a doctor or clinic to see if there is a remedy they can offer. But eventually the answer is in Christ.

> *"And when Zacharias saw him, he was troubled, and fear fell upon him. But the angel said unto him, Fear not, Zacharias: for thy prayer is heard; and thy wife..." (Luke 1:11-13).*

God did this because Elisabeth was born for a purpose and her womb was barren until she came unto her destiny and that is to birth the forerunner of Christ into this world.

All of us have a purpose and destiny to fulfill. We just don't know until we walk in the commandments and ordinances of the Lord.

In spite of Sarai and Elisabeth being barren, they were still able to become mothers in their late years which we consider beyond the child bearing age. Even though this happened in different dispensations of time, the answer was the same for this type situation. They both walked in God's ways and obeyed God in all his commandments. We cannot say today that our wives who are barren are walking in God's commandments. Many of the husbands and wives today that find themselves not fruitful are not worshipping God. And when they become worshipers of God, they will get the same result as Sarai and Elisabeth.

On the other hand, we as husbands and wives forget about trying to conceive and go out an adopt children so that we can become fathers and mothers. God's plan is for every married couple to have children so as to replenish the earth.

Ironically, Paul wrote a passage of scriptures to the Galatians' church saying rejoice thou barren that bearest not, break forth the cry, thou that travailest not for the desolate hath many more children than she which hath an husband.

In this passage it has been prophesied that the single mothers will have more children than the married mothers. I found this to be somewhat true in our day and time. There are many single mothers with three or more children than a mother that is married which seems to have one or two children.

CHAPTER 18

Roles of the Believer/ Disciple/Christian/Saint

In my first book, I had mentioned about being a believer, disciple, Christian, and/or saint. The terms and roles of each are incorporated in each other. A believer is one that believes in God Almighty and his Son Jesus Christ. He is one that has received water baptism and the Holy Ghost baptism in the name of Jesus. This term is clearly defined in Mark (16:17-18):

> *"And these signs shall follow them that believe: In my name shall they cast out devils; they shall speak with new tongues; They shall take up serpents; and if they drink any deadly thing, it shall not hurt them; they shall lay hands on the sick, and they shall recover,"*

In other words, a believer shall as the scriptures say have the five signs following him or noted in his or her life's living.

A disciple is one who believes and follows the teaching of Jesus Christ. He has eliminated all other Gods and is now accepting specific teaching from his God's doctrine and creed. In other words a disciple is a follower of the teaching of his Master and/or God. Moreover, he is a student learning his Master's doctrine. Jesus is our Master and we're following Him via his Word.

A Christian is a disciple who has matured in the teaching of Jesus to the point that one or more of the spiritual gifts and/or spiritual fruit will be manifested in his or her life to perform specific work(s) for Jesus. He is striving to master the teachings and to perfect his life's living.

The spiritual gifts are found in I Corinthians (12:1-11):

> *"But the manifestation of the Spirit is given to every man to profit withal. For to one is given by the Spirit the word of wisdom; to another the word of knowledge by the same Spirit; To another faith by the same Spirit; to another the gifts of healing by the same Spirit; To another the working of miracles; to another prophecy; to another discerning of spirits; to another divers kinds of tongues; to another the interpretation of tongues..."*

The spiritual fruit is found in Galatians (5:22-23) and as follows:

> *"But the fruit of the Spirit is love, joy, peace, longsuffering, gentleness, goodness, faith, Meekness, temperance: against such there is no law."*

A saint is a Christian who has matured in the Word of God and has no sin in his or her life. He has reached perfection and living a sinless life. His or her work is just about nearing completion on the earth and he or she is ready to exit this world. For instance, as Paul has reached perfection and nearing the end of his mission, he informed his friend Timothy of this. For he said in II Timothy (4:6-8), I am ready to be offered, and the time of my departure is at hand. I have fought a good fight. I have finished my course. I have kept the faith. Henceforth there is laid up for me a crown of righteousness which the Lord, the righteous judge, shall give me at that day: and not to me only, but unto all them also that love his appearing.

Now that we have reviewed the terms so widely used today in the Christendom, women's roles will forever be increased if she decides to become a child of God. Being a child of God, means that she who is a believer, or Disciple, or Christian, and/or Saint must obey the Word of God that is of his/her Master. From a believer to the saint, there are numerous roles to be fulfilled by a child of God. Jesus in Luke (6:46-49) says,

> *"And why call ye me Lord, Lord, and do not the thing which I say? Whosoever cometh to me, and heareth my sayings, and doeth them, I will shew you to whom he is like: He is like a man..."*

In other words, we cannot do any of the roles of the believer, disciple, Christian, and saint unless we obey the Word of God. This is the initial role of a believer, to believe what God has said and/or written and execute it to the best of his ability. In John (1:40-51) is a passage of scripture that shows believers obeying the word of God or Jesus:

> *"One of the two which heard John speak, and followed him, was Andrew, Simon Peter's brother. He first findeth his own brother Simon, and saith unto him, We have found the Messias, which is being interpreted, the Christ. And he brought him to Jesus..."*

Thus, the first role of the believer is to obey and follow Christ. As you have seen in this passage of scripture, the disciples who were called by Christ obeyed. Today, we could not obey unless we obey him through the Word. This is why Jesus said,

> *"Why call me Lord and obey not what I have commanded you?"*

Other roles of the believer as found in the scriptures are recorded in the Book of Acts (2:38, 41-47): Peter had preached his first sermon on the day of Pentecost and at the end of it. His hearers asked him and the disciples, what must they do to be saved?

> *"Then Peter said unto them, Repent, and be baptized every one of you in the name of Jesus Christ for the remission of sins, and ye shall receive the gift of the Holy Ghost. Then they gladly received his word were baptized: and the same day there were added unto them..."*

From this recorded passage, we can visualize many roles of the believer such as: obeying the Word of God, living for Christ and not self, fellowshipping with one another, adding believers to the church, working signs and wonders, sharing the word, being faithful, doing the works of Christ, and baptizing the believers.

Again, Acts (3:1-8) recorded an instance whereby the disciples are doing other roles of the believer:

> *"Now Peter and John went up together into the temple at the hour of Prayer, being the ninth hour. And a certain man lame from his mother's womb was carried, whom they laid daily at the gate of the temple which is called Beautiful..."*

As a result, Peter and John demonstrated several roles of the believer: doing the works of Christ, healing and delivering, working signs and wonders, and helping a brother.

Furthermore, Acts (8:5-17) records this instance of more believers' roles:

> *"Then Philip went down to the city of Samaria, and preached Christ unto them. And the people with one accord gave heed unto those things which Philip spake, hearing and seeing the miracles which he did. For unclean spirits, crying with loud voices, came out of many that were possessed with them: and many taken with palsies, and that were lame, were healed. But when they believed Philip preaching the things concerning the kingdom of God, and the name of Jesus Christ, they were baptized, both men and women..."*

Several roles of the believer were executed by the disciples in this passage: speaking the Word, living for Christ, doing the works of Christ, healing and delivering, working signs and wonders, adding believers to the church, baptizing the believers, being a conduit for God's blessings, sharing the Word via witnessing, fellowshipping with others, praying and singing praises to God, helping a brother, and being faithful.

Consequently, there are many roles of the believer a man will take on as he grows in grace and knowledge. The listing is not all inconclusive, but sufficient enough to give you an idea of what's required by God of man. Just to reiterate the roles for you, here is a listing that man will engage in being a believer, disciple, Christian, and/or saint:

"Do the works of Christ,"
"Share the Word via witnessing,"
"Be faithful,"
"Fellowship with other believers,"
"Love one another,"
"Obey the Word of God,"
"Live for Christ and not self,"
"Be your brother's keeper,"
"Look out for others,"
"Be a mentor,"
"Draw others to Christ,"
"Forgive and forget by-gone,"
"Provide things honestly,"
"Be a conduit for God's blessings,"
"Speak the Word,"
"Heal and deliver,"
"Work signs and wonders,"
"Witness the Resurrection,"
"Distribute to the needy,"
"Help thy brother,"
"Add believers to the church,"
"Pray & sing praises to God,"
"Baptize the believers,"
"Fight not against God,"
"Guide sinners in the knowledge of God,"
"Live so the anointing matures,"
"Assure all things in common,"
"Be of one heart and soul,"
"Be counted worthy to suffer for his name,"

Similarly, God has functional roles for man as well as being a believer, disciple, Christian, and saint. And they are found in Ephesians (4:11-13),

> *"And he gave some, apostles; and some prophets; and some, evangelists; and some pastors and teachers; For the perfecting of the saints, for the work of the ministry, for the edifying of the body of Christ: Till we all come in the unity of the faith, and of*

> *the knowledge of the Son of God unto a perfect man, unto the measure of the stature of the fullness of Christ:"*

Not all men would assume these functional roles, but God will call numerous ones to fulfill them as needed. He (Jesus) called the twelve and lost only one, Judas Iscariot. Peter and the rest of the disciples cast lot to replace Judas' bishoprick, and the lot fell on Matthias. These all became known as the twelve apostles. Paul later on called himself an apostle because he did the work of an apostle. I Timothy (1:7) confirmed Paul's confession,

> *"Whereunto I am ordained a preacher, and an apostle, (I speak the truth in Christ, and lie not;) a teacher of the Gentiles in faith and verity."*

What are the qualifications to be an apostle? Acts (1:20-22) says,

> *"For it is written in the book of Psalms, let his habitation be desolate, and let no man dwell therein: and his bishoprick let another take. Wherefore of these men which have companied with us all the time that the Lord Jesus went in and out among us, Beginning from..."*

An apostle is a man who is divinely commissioned to represent our Lord Jesus Christ. His functions include performing miracles, preaching the gospel, witnessing of Christ's resurrection, writing scriptures, establishing Churches, interpreting prophecy, defending the truth, exposing heretics, and upholding discipline. Paul being an apostle established churches, wrote scriptures, preached the gospel, performed miracles, witnessed of Christ's resurrection, defended the truth, exposed heretics and upheld discipline. Yet, he was not a "called apostle." He did the works of an apostle, but his calling was to become a teacher of God.

A prophet of God is one that defines God's will and predicts the future. They are the visionaries for the church and members and predictors of the churches of impending danger. For example, the prophet Agabus came down to Caesarea and entered the house of

Philip the evangelist, which was one of the seven deacons and abode with him. Philip had four daughters who were also prophetesses that did prophesy. Paul was also at Philip's house. Acts (21:10-11) records a function of the prophet,

> *"And as we tarried there many days, there came down from Judaea a certain prophet, named Agabus. And when he was come unto us, he took Paul's girdle..."*

Agabus had earlier prophesied to the church about great dearth throughout the world that came to pass in the days of Claudius Caesar, (Acts 11:27-28). A true prophet is when his predictions come true. We have heard of many false prophets also.

An evangelist is one who proclaims the gospel in areas where the gospel has not been preached. His function is to convert the sinners and place them with the pastors and teachers. He revives the lost as to say. One such evangelist was Philip who was first made a deacon in the early church and later exalted by God to an evangelistic function. Acts (21:8) records this for us,

> *"And the next day we that were of Paul's company departed, and came unto Caesarea: and we entered into the house of Philip the evangelist, which was one of the seven; and abode with him."*

We see in Acts (8:5-8) where Philip carried out his evangelistic work for God:

> *"Then Philip went down to the city of Samaria, and preached Christ unto them. And the people with one accord gave heed unto those things which Philip spake, hearing and seeing the miracles which he did. For unclean spirits, crying with loud voices, came out of many that were possessed with them: and many taken with palsies, and that were lame, were healed. And there was great joy in that city."*

A pastor is a bishop or shepherd who cares for the members of the church. He sees after the day-to-day operation of the church. The qualifications for a pastor are recorded in I Timothy (3:1-7) and Titus (1:5-9) respectively:

> *"This is a true saying, If a man desire the office of a bishop, he desireth a good work. A bishop then must be blameless, the husband of one wife, vigilant, sober, of good behaviour, given to hospitality, apt to teach; Not given to wine, no striker, not a brawler, not covetous..."*

> *"For a bishop must be blameless, as the steward of God; not selfwilled, not soon angry, not given to wine, no striker, not given to filthy lucre; But a lover of hospitality, a lover of good men, sober, just, holy, temperate; Holding fast..."*

There were many churches in individuals' houses and those individuals over their homes were looked upon as the pastor or bishop. For examples: Paul said in Colossians (4:10-12,15),

> *"... Epaphras, who is one of you, a servant of Christ, saluteth you, always labouring fervently for you in prayers, that ye may stand perfect and complete in all the will of God. Salute the brethren which are in Laodicea, and Nymphas, and the church which is in his house."*

There were others who had churches in their homes as Paul made reference to in Philemon (1-2):

> *"Paul, a prisoner of Jesus Christ, and Timothy our brother, unto Philemon our dearly beloved, and fellowlabourer, And to our beloved Apphia, and Archippus our fellowsoldier, and to the church in thy house:"*

A teacher is one that instructs in God's way, God's path, and God's law. He is one that has been empowered by the Spirit and taught by God. He also has a divine calling. Acts (13:1-2) records a passage for our edification,

> *"Now there were in the church that was at Antioch certain prophets and teachers; as Barnabas, and Simeon that was called*

Niger, and Lucius of Cyrene and Manaen, which had been brought up with Herod the tetrarch, and Saul."

Paul, as I alluded to earlier, was a called teacher and also Barnabas. Acts (15:35) gives us information that they were teachers:

"Paul and Barnabas continued in Antioch, teaching and preaching the word of the Lord, with many others also."

Likewise, there are positional roles of the church a man or woman will assume. But women are not to hold such positions as Apostles, Pastors, Evangelists, and Teachers. But each individual is called in one calling and one election. The positional roles of man in the church are found in I Corinthians (12:27-28),

"Now ye are the body of Christ, and members in particular. And God hath set some in the church, first apostles, secondarily prophets, thirdly teachers, after that miracles, then gifts of healings, helps, governments, diversities of tongues."

This is not your local congregational church like we are accustomed to attending, but the spiritual church ofJesus Christ. These eight positions make up the body ofJesus Christ. They are scattered throughout the world because the body of Jesus is global. Jesus has to elect you to one of these positions. Then it is up to you to make your calling and election sure.

"Wherefore the rather, brethren, give diligence to make your calling and election sure: for if ye do these things, ye shall never fall:" (II Peter 1:10)

Again, not all of mankind will assume the functional and positional roles of man. But there'll be some who would not even do the basic roles of man such as work or do labor. As you can obtain from this writing that there are a lot of roles which man must perform from day to day in order to live and give God Glory. God expects every man to give him some glory.

Lightning Source UK Ltd.
Milton Keynes UK
UKHW041019110219
337097UK00001B/222/P

9 781546 275428